The Universal Law of Creation:

"When You Seek, Ask, See and Truly Believe Beyond Any Shadow—of—a—Doubt Whatsoever, You Shall Receive!"

Secrets and Laws of the UNIVERSE

Scribed by Gino DiCaprio

Secrets and Laws of the Universe

Scribed by **Gino DiCaprio**

Publisher: **Motivational Press, Inc.**

The publisher may be contacted at: www.motivationalpress.com/

Credits:

Chief Editor by: **Gino DiCaprio**

Project Manager by: **Justin Sachs**

Project Assistant by: **Gino Iovannone**

Cover—Design and Book design by: **Alfredo Jorge**

Composition and Design by: **Gino DiCaprio**

Edited by: **Shoshana Kalfon**

Proof—Reading by: **Enrique Guerrero**, **Shirley Meier** and **Shoshana Kalfon**

www.facebook.com/UniversalLawOfCreation

Disclaimer

The information contained in this paper book is an opinion, or collection of opinions, and it should be used for personal entertainment purposes only. You are responsible for your own behavior, and none of this paper book is to be considered legal, personal advice. The material is provided, as is, without warranty of any kind, either express or implied. Motivational Press, Inc. does not warrant, guarantee, or make any representations regarding the use, or the results of the use, of the web sites, products, services audio or written materials in the terms of correctness, accuracy, reliability, currentness or otherwise. The entire risk as to the results and performance of the web sites, products and services are assumed by you. If the web sites, products, services audio or written materials are defective, you, and not Motivational Press, Inc., assume the entire cost of all necessary servicing, repair or correction. Motivational Press, Inc. its owners, suppliers, employees, affiliates, presenters, producers and participants, will not be liable for any damages whatsoever that may result from making use of the activities, advice or information contained herein, including without limitation, damages for loss of business profits, business interruption, loss of business information, or other pecuniary loss.

To contact Mr. DiCaprio for an Event for public speaking or private is under info@MotivationalPress.com

Where quotations or notes have been used, permission has been sought. Where this has been possible to obtain, we would like to apologize and, if notified will correct the omission in future editions.

Contents

CONTENTS

Introduction

"If you find it in your heart to care for somebody else, you will have succeeded." — **Maya Angelou**

You all know that there are different parts at the beginning of books called the "*Foreword*," "*Preface*," "*Acknowledgement*," and "*Introduction*."

I wrote everything in this book with the help of a Higher Source. I am not only seeking people who agree with my point of view but also those who do not believe, or else I shall learn nothing. Finding those with opposing views and asking what if they may be right is a learning experience. It is beneficial that both sides keep an open—mind about different ideas and philosophies.

I understand that you may feel the urge to skip over to another page or chapter in an attempt to cut to the chase. However, I will tell you to fight off that desire because everything you read will be important. If you give your full attention from the start of this book to the very end of it, you will have a much better chance of succeeding and achieving your objective(s). I am not about suppressing your thoughts; I am here to help you surpass them.

This is an all—in—one formula. I hope that while you digest my book(s) you will use it/them as your own personal guide in all aspects of your life. My formula should be used as a reference tool for meeting the opposite sex, being successful in relationships, controlling your emotions, acquiring financial success, as well as a way to Spiritually Intertwine yourself with the Universe so you can follow the "*Ancient Universal Law of Creation*".

> *"People may ask what dating has to do with the Power of the Universe. When 'picking up' women, you must have confidence and you must believe that you will succeed in the goal. When you believe in something so much, you make it come true. That is the Power of the Universe. This shows how the Universe intertwines with dating, relationships, and every aspect of life."*

That's how my son Aaron explains it to his Pépé.[1]

I recently came back home from a U.S. Detention Faculty[2] with my written notes in hand. I shall be using some of these notes in this book. I arrived home to my kids on February 8th 2010 after a three year absence. Writing this book, as well as others, was a turning point for me. Being away was an opportunity for me to reflect on my life, what it was up until that point, and decide what I wanted it to be from that point forward.

I am assuming you singled out this book because you are at a turning point in your own life. Maybe you are dissatisfied with how you deal with "*life*" in general and believe there must be a way of improving your life. Maybe you received the "*Calling*".

Congratulations, if this is true, you have picked up the right book! If not, then please go pick up a magazine! I am not stating that you will find all your answers here. But this will be a start to your quest.

If you are going to read this book to improve your life and apply what is of value to your life, then this book will change your life. If

1 Grandfather from his mother's side

2 I was wrongly accused of crimes by the U.S. and Canadian Federal Government. I was in a detention center for crimes I didn't commit when I wrote these books, and it took me over seven years to prove my innocence. For five years I fought while I was on house arrest (2003—2007), reporting on a weekly basis to the RCMP ... and for two and a half years (2007—2010) from outside my country in a U.S. Detention Center, far from my loved ones in Quebec, Canada. I was acquitted of all charges. What I teach, I practice, and have proven, works.

you are just "*browsing*," if you are just "*curious*" then do not waste your time, and I hope you kept the receipt. If it is in an "*E—Format*" then delete it or if it is in "*Paper Format*" return it back to the store where you purchased it, or give it—to—someone who is not afraid to embrace a better life. If this upsets you, that's life. Very cocky and unwarranted sarcasm…not needed.[3]

Although you may be unhappy, others may pressure you to stay right where you are. However, deep inside you, you sense things are off—balance. If those close to you disapprove of your quest to make changes, you are most likely to keep doing what you are currently doing. The longer you have lived a certain way, the harder it is to change the way. The harder it is to forget and learn a new way.

What does it mean to satisfy ones self?

You know what you do not "*like*" but you do not know how to think of, much less find, a fulfilling alternative. This book will help you see yourself change, which in turn, will affect everything you do in every aspect of your life. Once you finish reading this book, you will be better suited to put all that you have learned to good use.

I would like to tell you a little about my personal background by explaining to you how I became involved in "*Spiritual Teaching*".

After my five and a half year relationship with my girlfriend ended in September 2007, I was lost; the relationship did not end well. I did not follow my own teachings and was both embarrassed and ashamed. I had ended my previous relationship of sixteen years with my wife Shoshana, the mother of my three beautiful children, in a positive way. In this relationship, however, I was not a part of the decision to end it.

3 Need shows poverty. "In my book it is giving away your power."

A month after my break—up with my girlfriend, with the support of my former wife, and one day before I had to leave in October 2007[4], I found out that having my heart broken by my ex—girlfriend was my way to wholeness. After my life fell apart, I became open to new dimensions of my existence that I had denied for years, yet they were just waiting for my recognition. It was hard for me to see this when I was in terrible pain, however when I finally looked back upon my life, I discovered that another door of unlimited possibility had just opened for me. Soon after this event, I had to leave my home.

The reason I had to leave my home and family was that I was caught in a conspiracy. This was "*dismissed*" a few years later because of lack of proof.

I am "*Gino DiCaprio*" formerly known as "*Jake Hollow*".

I wrote "*The Jake Hollow Guide on How to Persuade Women*" plus (Revised Edition) and "*How to Deal with Emotions and the Life of a Motivational Speaker*"[5] under my old stage name Jake Hollow. More than anything, those books deal with the old physical ego aspect of me. I wrote them between November 2007 and April 2008 before I awoke to my real Spiritual—Self[6] which I began writing between May and July 2008.

My work that is written under my previous stage name Jake Hollow was mostly written by me and some by my Higher—Self, nevertheless most of my Gino DiCaprio work was mostly written by my Higher Self

4 Refer to "The Jake Hollow Guide on How to Persuade Women." (Revised Edition) Introduction section

5 Published by Motivational Press, Inc.

6 My full awakening was at the end of October 2007 when I called my former wife Shoshana about my visions of December 2012, where I stood on stage with all these religious (High Priest) from every belief, over looking billion of people, praying in their upbringing traditions.

that took over my physical body while in trance with the help of my Spiritual Guide.

Around that time, I was training select prison inmates who wanted to change their lives. They succeeded, with my assistance. I became an inspiration to many inmates and C.Os[7] on staying positive, being sure and confident about oneself, without worries. A few of these inmates are now interested in becoming Life—Coaches or Spiritual Teachers. Some lacked confidence and I helped them rebuild that; they now have the hope that they can achieve change. That is what they truly wanted. My words seemed to soothe them and give them unbelievable hope and confidence. I was referred to as "*Master DiCaprio*" or "*Mi—L—rd DiCaprio*" the High Adamant Counsellor and Advisor.[8]

I have become a stronger man because of that experience; stronger than I was before. Being in this type of place (*detention center*) can only do one of two things to you. It can "*break*" or "*make*" you. It has made me who I am. Fate has chosen this path for me.

Now, however, I highly recommend that you read this book more than once. Do not miss even one page and by this, I mean from front to back cover and then slowly re—read "*ALOUD*" each paragraph each day until it sinks deeply into you;

Why?

There are secret hidden codes in my pages.[9] Taking notes will help deepen the meaning in your mind. So make this a fun activity even though this is a serious journey.

What is the point of living if you are not having fun enjoying life?

7 Correctional Officers
8 Inside joke by the way while I would laugh it off
9 If you have the "Calling", the "Gift" from the Spiritual Realm

Please Note: Only you can stop yourself from moving forward. These books should not be read silently, but "*ALOUD*" and each paragraph should, at some stage, be analyzed closely and personally.

When you read, I want you to feel it as if I am "*speaking directly to you*" and that I am "*putting you into a trance*".

I tell you, the reader, that you have two options:

To read it as if it is an ordinary book and not get the full force of the power available to you,

or

Do what I recommend as a requirement and read it aloud with passion as if reading it to a captivated audience who is hanging on your every word!

This book should be read with commitment and a feeling of greatness and energy.

You are to imagine your audience listening to each word carefully, feeding off the words, wanting to hear each word, wanting more, as they all lean forward in their seats, absolutely entranced.

As the reader, you should visualize yourself standing on a stage, book in one hand, with the other arm free to gestulate, as you walk around the stage, reading the book aloud and with great passion!

Acknowledgement

"Through our willingness to help others, we can learn to be happy rather than depressed." — **Gerald Jampolsky**

I would like to first thank my lovely, beautiful, and elegant best friend and former wife ... Shoshana, for her heartfelt loyalty towards me as well as the tremendous sacrifices she has made to help me by still being there for and raising our three beautiful children. Her contribution to the quality of this book has been immeasurable. She and I do not always agree on my view in life, but we do compromise in how my words should be used in my book. My gratitude to all who have been here for me is very sincere.

I have not always treated her fairly over the years, and yet, she has remained supportive and present. Regardless of my behaviour, she has proven herself stronger than either of us could have imagined.

She has stood by me when no one else would. Not out of necessity or obligation. She was there for me, even after our divorce, when my life took several negative turns. This required that I confront and acknowledge my wrongdoings and, to some extent, prove my actual role in unfortunate circumstances. I have paid dearly for my mistakes; however, I have very little regret for the time I have had to spend paying for my discretions in detention centers in both Canada and the United States. These experiences have helped me focus and re—evaluate myself: how I behave, how I think, and how I treat and have treated others. In addition, my experiences have given me the opportunity to write the book you are now reading.

My biggest regrets, however, are missing my son's Bar—Mitzvah[10] and my children's birthdays. These are moments and experiences in my children's lives that I have lost and they have suffered from my absence.

I wish to express my sincerest appreciation, as well as my heartfelt gratitude, to my three gorgeous and bright children. I want to thank my son, Aaron and my twin daughters, Ariel and Leila, for always being there for me, especially after my last break—up with Jezebel. This hurt them emotionally.[11] They have been my greatest supporters and I cannot love them more than I do at this moment. I now understand that they, and their mother, love me unconditionally. More than I could have ever realized.

None of my work endeavours will overshadow the supreme importance of my family. I spend my energy on my loved ones, an investment that will have an abundantly fortifying return. They are my core reason for being.

I would also like to thank my mother (Maria) for not giving up on me when I was going through these difficult emotional and Spiritual moments.

I want to credit those who have helped edit this book and who have given their opinion on keeping it real and not losing its message. Therefore, I want to thank Enrique Guerrero, Shirley Meier and ex—wife Shoshana for their contribution.

I also must thank others who, near the end of this book, inspired me. They allowed my philosophy on life and my love to help them

10 According to Jewish law, when Jewish children reach the ages of thirteen for boys and twelve for girls, they become responsible for their actions, and "become a Bar or Bat Mitzvah" (English: Son (Bar) or Daughter (Bat) of the commandments)

11 Refer to Jake Hollow's "How to Deal with Emotions and the Life of a Motivational Speaker," Part I: Life—Coaches on Internal Damage, Chapter 3: Who Am I?, Subtitle "IV My Pain, My Calling."

in their lives. I wish to thank Roman Brave,[12] whom I have known for over thirty years and Ivaylo Marinov, who I have known for over eighteen years.

I would also like to acknowledge Diablo Santana[13] and Mike Thomas.[14] I had the privilege of meeting them in Rivière—des—Prairie Institution (*RDP*) in Montréal, Québec. In addition Lennin (*Choco*) Anaya, Reuben Porcher, Ernst (*Miami*) Appolon, Jason (*Minx*) Robinson, Jonathan (*Big Worm*) Campbell, Christian Biancardi, Michael J. Morse, and Anthony Morse from the Donald W. Wyatt Detention Facility (DWWDF) in Central Falls, Rhode Island. They have each taken the time to read a portion of my book and offer their remarks of strong encouragement and constructive criticism.

I have asked myself for years,

Why am I here?

The answer has always been in front of me. People of all ages always came to me for advice. My teachers told me I should have been a counsellor, as did Shoshana.

However, it took two strangers, one from my own city[15] and the other from San Diego, to see my true calling, my true potential.

It took a correctional institution to wake me up. I wrote, and as a result, many inmates opened their eyes and their ears to my teachings.

12 Up—and coming Life—Coach
13 Up—and coming Seduction—Coach
14 One of the former owners of UFC
15 Montréal

They became aware and they awoke. Some say I have built a following, yet they are not followers. They did not become proud, for what I have offered is not from me, but a Higher Source.

You will say to me; "*What I've read means whatever you want or require it to mean.*" NO! It means what it means.

My being incarcerated made me think hard about "*life*" so that I will make the right decisions to lead a better lifestyle. This enables me to be free.

Additionally, in prison, there is no noise or tumult to disturb one as there is in free society. This helped me think clearly and honestly about improving my life without disturbances.

— —

Please Note: Expressing myself, either verbally or in writing, has never been my strength (I jumble my words, I misspell). What I want to say or express, the concepts and ideas, the thoughts, the suggestions, the meaning behind my words, however, has been, and still is, my strongest ability. I'm difficult to understand, especially when I speak. How I articulate and annunciate my words are not as clear as they are when I write. Writing allows me to think, and express myself, in a clearer fashion. Although this is very true, my audience seems to appreciate this quality about me (they say it makes me more real and believable). Writing has helped me express myself more creatively and clearly, thus improving my memory and precision, as well as other aspects of my performance when teaching to a live audience.

ACKNOWLEDGEMENT

I was born in France but grew up in Montreal. My parents are Italian; I was raised a Catholic, but then became a Jehovah Witness. In my late 20's, I converted to Judaism and settled into Jewish history. Following that, I have studied all beliefs from Buddhism to Islam. At this point in my life, I am more aware of "Spiritual Consciousness" as I feel that all beliefs have some truth to them and I consider them as one.

I do not believe in a G—d since there are many g—ds. I believe there is an Original entity that is above "*ALL G—ds*" who I call by many names.

Being in a detention facility made me aware of my inner—self. Now I know my path, my true path. Now I know I can achieve whatever I want.

It also allowed me to see myself for who I was in the past and who I am now with full understanding.

I move to work, not work to move. There is no such thing as luck. You make your fortune on thoughts and hard smart work, never luck. Believing in luck is giving away your power. I, on the other hand, control my power, with the Universe beside me.

The Ancient Universal Law of Creation has many more laws underneath it. I was aware of this Power before I heard of Rhonda Byrne's book on the "*Law of Attraction*."

On Sunday, March 7th, 2010, I finally watched a part of "*The Secret*" on "*YouTube.com*" and I was amazed to see that what it talked about was, word for word, what I was writing about in my book. This was before I saw or read her work and heard comments from those who were in her video. I became aware of a similar perspective on the views presented on this page when observing the work done in "*The Secret*" by Ronda Byrne.

It is amazing how we are each connected. When I was originally writing my book in a Detention Facility, my work was being compared to that of James Redfield, author of "*The Celestine Prophecy*" and Rhonda Byrne, author of "*The Secret*". I still have not read their books but plan to read them one day. At the moment I do not want to be influenced by other peoples work, until after my books are published. This way I cannot be accused of plagiarism. The book that motivated me in this belief was by Wallace Delois Wattles,[16] author of "The Science of Getting Rich" written in 1910.

Thank you

Peace and Love

Gino

16 He passed away in 1911

Prologue

"It isn't that they can't see the solution. It is that they can't see the problem." — **G.K. Chesterton**

I realized, after I started writing my books back in November 2007, that I had underestimated my calling, so around July 2008 my focus changed. I was no longer interested in my original topics[17] on seducing women since it made me look as if I was teaching guys to become "*con—men*" and instead of teaching how to respect women.

My new view on life showed the amount of work it would require of me to complete my work as being more intensive than I thought it would be. It became clear to me that I would be required to take this seriously and concentrate all my energies fully on my calling in life as my most important goal and not as an afterthought.

I grew up having no confidence in every area of my life. I did not know how to read or write, make a living, hold on to money, have a relationship, or even how to date women. One day, I decided to change my life; I grew my hair long[18] and, as a result, my hair became the foundation of who I was then and who I am now. Therefore, as they say, the rest is history. So, if you believe I do not understand where you are coming from, think again.

17 Jake Hollow's "How to Deal with Emotions and the Life of a Motivational Speaker," Part I: Life—Coaches on Internal Damage, Chapter 4: Jake's Interviews

18 As in the biblical story of Samson (Shimshon)

My life is about thinking and being neutral—positive;[19] I am always thinking in a positive way. I believe anything is possible. How you operate daily when it comes to achieving what you "*really*" want in life is extremely important. So think big, think positive, and do it daily. Even if you are in prison or near death, be positive. You are a "*survivor*" and that means that you must look at obstacles as challenges that must be overcome and not as problems without solutions.

Here is an illustration:

I want to open an office in Japan. I send you over there for a three week stay to study the market for any obstacles that may prevent this new business venture from growing. I put you on a first class flight, have you stay in a five star hotel, and provide you with a Platinum Credit Card to buy whatever you require. My expectation is that you will come back with a list of challenges and solutions so that I can begin my business venture. You, on the other hand, come back three weeks later telling me that Japan is "not" a good market to begin a new business venture. You only saw obstacles and, therefore, could not find solutions to these "problems."

Be honest…if you were in my shoes...

How would you handle this?

Personally, I would fire you on the spot!

Why?

Why would I waste my money sending you to Japan, buying you a first class ticket with all expense paid for entertainment, restaurants,

19 Or as Alfredo Jorge calls it "Balance"

and the best hotels if I believed deep inside me that there was no market there?

You looked at this trip[20] as a "*problem*" with no solutions while I wanted a "*solution*" to the challenges that existed but surmountable.

Now, let us say that I send another person on this same trip. This person chooses to return "*earlier*" than expected with, however, a list of solutions to work with so that my business will do well there. See the difference?

I learned this approach from the "*Torah*" when Moshe[21] sent spies into the "*Promise Land;*"[22] they, however, turned into "*problem focused*" (**negative**) spies. They saw giants that could not be defeated and an enemy that was too powerful. In essence, an insurmountable force, forcing them to wander forty years in the desert because they were afraid of invading the land believing the people there were too powerful. Yet, forty years later, it took Yeshua[23] to complete the invasion with "*solution focused*" (**positive**) spies who found ways to defeat the perceived enemy.

The point is that you must always work to find a solution when an obstacle comes before you. When you work to find a solution, it comes. In other words, you must not look at something as a problem too difficult to deal with. Better yet, another way to look at it is to take care of the issue before it becomes a problem.

20 As a vacation to enjoy

21 Hebrew and Aramaic for Moses

22 Translit: ha—Aretz ha—Muvtachat. Was given to their descendants and was described in terms of the territory from the River of Egypt to the Euphrates river. The land of the Kenites, Kenizzites, Kadmonites, Hittites, Perizzites, Rephaites, Amorites, Canaanites, Girgashites and Jebusites.

23 Joshua. Hebrews: Yehoshua; same as Jesus; Latin: Josue or Jesus in Hebrews; Arabic: Yusha' ibn Nūn. Joshua's name was Hoshea the son of Nun, of the tribe of Ephraim, but that Moses called him Joshua.

With Jezebel, I had a moderate relationship; yet, I was in love with her. I lost her, nevertheless. I allowed fearful thoughts of losing her to enter my mind, until that fearful thought of loss became my dominant thought. I tipped the scale from thinking thoughts of a strong relationship to thinking thoughts of loss and I lost her. Furthermore, I realized that deep in my subconsciousness, I could not really commit myself to her, yet I could not end it. As I have said, I recently went through some very negative and unfortunate circumstances. This was the lowest and worst time of my life. Now, however, the fear of loss is gone; nothing will scare me as much as this recent experience. As a result, I am tipping the scale back to who I really am.

Now, my thought is that no one controls what my life will be other than me. I shall never lose myself or think negatively again because it is okay to fear; it is not okay, however, to let fear control you. Control your fear by transforming it into a positive thing. I have seen and lived this personally. I have learned to use my fear and cause positive outcomes. I have done this with others, as well.

This was not always the case, however. I knew my last relationship would end and that it would not end well. In 2005, I told my then girlfriend how we would break—up and it happened exactly how, as well as, when I said it would happen in 2007. In reality, I created the "*breaking—up*" situation well before it happened. If you see it in your mind, you are going to have it in front of you — both good and bad.[24]

You shall notice, throughout my book, I use the term the "*Universe*" however you can change it to whatever belief you want from "*Creator, G—d, Higher Being, Maker, Spirit, Universal Consciousness*", and "*Yahweh*" and the list goes on. Use which ever term makes you more comfortable in the end.

24 Book II: Time is an Illusion

BOOK I:

Secrets and Laws of the Universe

CHAPTER 1

Logic and Belief

"If you seek to understand the whole Universe, you will understand nothing at all. If you seek only to understand your Self, you will understand the whole Universe." — **Anonymous**

This book deals with life, in general. It shows you how to be at peace with yourself, how to accept that you have total control over your existence, and how you control your own perception of reality along with who truly controls it. I am what people consider a Spiritual Teacher who teaches you how to connect and create whatever you want. Although most of you[25] seem unable to connect or create whatever you want, it is your birthright to command it. It all has to do with a Secret Society that entered our civilizations thousands of years ago.[26]

I have gone through a metamorphosis. I see myself with a clearer awareness of my Higher Divine—Self. My thoughts have changed and this has led the energy surrounding me to change. I am finally at peace, and I feel joy and harmony. I have gone on many Spiritual journeys by meditating through trancing.

25 Ninety—Seven percent.

26 Refer to "Book III: Illuminatis The Ones and The Shadows"

Only some have noticed my change; others may see it but don't say anything. Nonetheless, I see it happening and I am enjoying being blessed with this wonderful journey that I am on and hope to continue by not letting my ego—self take over again. It's like Mr. Spock of Star Trek (*if you follow it*) when he struggles to ignore his human feelings so that he can maintain his logical—Vulcan self.

I have become awakened to my Inner Light and am opening to new levels of Spiritual understanding and awareness. Remember that your understanding of being Spiritual may not relate to my understanding of it. Most people have this concept of Spirituality as expressed by Ghandi, Buddha or Jesus as peaceful. This was misunderstood by their followers and the masses. They lived Spiritual lives, attaching "*love*" to all of their thoughts, actions, and inspirations.

Do not misunderstand me; I do not feel that love should not be a part of the equation. Love of self and of others is the foundation for all that we do and all that we are as human beings.

The difference between how they express "*Spirituality*" and how I express it stems from my belief that "*love does not conquer all*" and it is not the direct solution to a problem. At times, being a "*Spiritual Warrior*" is what is warranted to solve a problem so that love can then solidify the solution.

What is the Truth?

The Truth is that the Truth is closer than you may believe. If you choose not to read further then it is your right since the choice is yours. You only choose to open yourself when you feel that you are ready. Do you agree?

When you read this book, please have an open—mind. Read between the lines that you read and capture the messages that I have made an effort to send you.

Throughout my book, I have put secret information in codes that only a select few should be able to decipher. In other words, only those with the gifts will be able to understand.

Am I getting this from my inner—self, a Higher Source, the Supreme Being, the Universe, G—d, or whatever you want to call it or from any other belief you may have?

I will leave the answer to you in your personal belief.

The message I receive I understand as a simple one. This makes my words all the more credible since I am not highly educated in worldly knowledge so I will not complicate things and will explain them simply. I will not compose elaborate sentences that would be difficult for many non—readers to read.

What is the Universal Law of Creation?

How does it work?

Are you willing to find it and understand it?

Tell me, as well as yourself;

Are you hungry for it?

Respond to this question aloud as if you were talking to me. After this, you can ask yourself;

Who am I?

You are a survivor; you are more than who you believe you are. You are stronger, wiser, more valuable, and much more than you know yourself to be. Any inability to accept who you are only holds back your full potential to be your true self. Even if you have studied every philosophical view out there, you still do not feel an improvement in your full potential. Am I right so far?

All the things that you believe to have gone wrong in your life are not what you believe them to be. Until you finally see the Truth I present to you, you will continue on that same path, so read on to extend your full potential.

Things that go wrong in your life are an opportunity.

To this statement, you will most likely answer back with;

> *Why would you state that what goes wrong with my life is an opportunity?*

The answer to this question is that life itself is working on "*clearing*" everything that has "*not*" been working for you. Yet you do not see it. Do you follow?

Life is just showing you how to re—start itself from scratch. Thanks to this, you will now have room to rebuild your life into "*what you really and truly want*".

I am not talking about any physical desire. I am talking about our True Spiritual thoughts in the Spiritual Realm that have plans and do not interfere with our physical dilemma. The True Higher You picked the physical life you are living to acquire knowledge. [27]

---

27 Refer to "Book II: Time is an Illusion"

Life is not about focusing on what you do not want. You must always focus on what you want, even if it means that you have to start over to achieve it. Whenever this beginning comes to be, you have the potential to be in the better life you selected.

What do you "truly" want?

What do you want your life to be?

If you are a person with little confidence, you most likely never truly made yourself want anything. Am I right? If not, then you are only lying to yourself.

You believe there are people in worse situations than you are, yet deep, deep inside you, you believe differently.

You feel you have nowhere to go.

If you feel this, let me tell you; you deserve another chance.

It can take a long time to accept this, but there are really good people out there who want to help you. Yet, you must first help yourself. If you cannot do this, then no one can do it for you.

You try[28] to convince people that you are independent and do not need[29] help. However, with the same breath you say, "No body helps me, they are focused on their life," am I correct on this?

It is not important to understand the details of why bad things happen to you. All you must understand is that bad things happen

28 Try is considered Lazy.
29 Need shows poverty. "In my book it is giving away your power."

for a reason. It can take a long time to accept this. You must first help yourself, only you can do this for yourself.

Now get back up, and get off that wide road you have been taking, and take the lost original narrow road that was always your path and your birthright.

The narrow road may seem dangerous yet it is not. In contrast, the wide road may seem faster and safer; however, it is not. The truth is, that road is just an illusion.[30]

Before Creation existed it had to Emanate.[31] This was the moment before creation when space and time did not exist in the physical reality, which is just an illusion. What I am about to reveal has been hidden in symbols for over hundreds of thousands of years.[32] In addition, every few thousand years "*WE*" share it with you, the mass population, yet only a selective few understand it. Only those who are in high positions, Spiritually, know about it, along with the few who have discovered it over the years. However, before I reveal more let me ask you,

Do you really believe this is the first time you have been in this physical realm?

All you have known about Spirituality is not what it really represents. What it truly represents cannot be explained in physical terms; you must become one with it to understand the True meaning of Spirituality. All that you have believed has been altered and tainted too much to create your reality.[33]

30 Refer to "Book I1: Time is an Illusion"
31 Emanate is the process before Creation starts.
32 Those who follow their religious belief assume Earth is only eleven thousand years old.
33 Refer to "Book II: Time is an Illusion"

What you want out of life is all up to you, do you agree? You must believe this fact with unconditional blind faith. You must think and visualize as real, all that you truly desire together with a mental image of your wishes and dreams. You must touch it, feel it, sense it, smell it, and taste it as if it were real. As a result, this authentic desire will be in front of you and not out of your reach. Alter your thoughts to link them in your reality. You must feel its existence unconditionally deep down in your heart. Believe in what you truly want without any doubt or even the shadow of a doubt. Believe totally that you already have what you want. Believe totally that you deserve it, and that it is all possible for you. Whatever you do, believe it always and do not give up by just saying;

This does not work.

If in the past you have given up. I will put my belief to the test and say that if you had persisted, and believed without any shadow—of—a—doubt whatsoever in your desire, you would have achieved your goal.

Why do I write this?

I write this so that you become aware that deep down in your subconscious mind, you have doubts and do not fully see or believe what you want to make your conscious mind believe. Then you will be able to shift your thoughts and train them like other muscles in your body.

Personally, I believe "*time*" and "*reality*" are just "*illusions*" that you "*created*," and caused "*to exist*". I have believed, and still believe, in this concept. It was my belief even before I heard of Albert Einstein's theory and his famous quote: "*Reality is merely an illusion*".[34]

34 Refer to "Book II: Time is an Illusion"

The past, present, and the so—called future are all one timeline; everything is happening simultaneously. Understand this as a fact. In reality, there is no time, so if you believe in what you want, then it already exists in your future. Therefore, as everything is happening at once, then there "*IS*" a version of you in a parallel reality that received what you really wanted and this reality exists.

Throughout my book, I will ask you to close your eyes at least once a day, just for several minutes, and visualize what you want, not what you do not want.[35] You must truly believe it unconditionally, as well as sense the feelings of already having what you want.

Feel grateful for what you already have and stay positive. Start your day, then release your wish to the Universe and trust that the Universal Consciousness will fully absorb and understand how to manifest your wish[36] creation.

Believe in the reality you created in your mind while having the feelings that belong to reality. Like this, your source, the Universe, will attract this reality and make it happen, just the way you defined it in your mind. This must not be a one time idea; do it everyday of your life, the same way you exercise your muscles.

Believe in your objective without any doubt or even the shadow of a doubt even if you have not yet physically achieved it. Do you follow? It may not happen overnight, yet it will happen. However, this will come to be not when you expect it to be, but when you least expect it to occur.

Imagine that you already have what you wish for; learn to play that game while making believe you have it until it physically materializes.

35 Refer to Subtitle "Chapter 4: Envisioning Your Ideas to Reality"

36 One thing I have learned is that this word should not be used. If you "wish" for things you will only have the experience of wishing and what you wish for will not materialize.

Make it fun. Feel it, feel good about it, and you will feel better about yourself. It will begin to flow into your life. The moment you have doubts, you must immediately move them out of your mind and replace them with "*positive thoughts*". This will change the outcome into what you want.

YES, I will repeat myself, throughout the contents of this book, so that what I write shall be ingrained in your being.

You will notice that I will always insist, quite rightly, that you, as an individual, must not take my word for everything I write, nor should you believe everything I teach. Instead, as should be done with any author, you, the readers, must take what you feel is relevant, or right. Always have an open mind, though, and do your own research.

Always feel happy, for you are emitting to the Universe your innermost thoughts and your life feelings that lie deep in your subconscious. Whatever you want must be feasible in your mind or it will not work. This is the reason why I always say; "*In my heart I truly believe without a doubt or even the shadow of a doubt whatsoever that I am...*" You can use this statement to express your own desires.

It is your job to "*Ask*," "*Seek*," "*See*," and "*Believe*" that you are "*Receiving*" and feel pleased and happy at the present moment. Do not worry about how you will receive your desires. Let the Universe worry about the "details" in how they will happen; do not let it be your concern.

Change your behaviour, repeat day and night continuously, like a parrot, that you can change your life. Visualize life, health, and wealth and how you want them and attach that to those around. Tell yourself; "*I CAN!*" and "*I WILL!*"

Make this your predominant thought for anything you want. Engrave in your mind that life, health, wealth, or/and a great social environment is not hard to attain. Believe it and immediately disregard any opposite ideas. This state of being comes from within, not from without. Say aloud, with true feelings; "*THERE'S AN ABUNDANCE OF JOY OUT THERE AND I CAN HAVE IT!*"

Some people are only focused on the greed of superabundance, yet abundance is much more than just material wealth. Abundance is the flow of energy that comes to you from the Universal Source of life, represented both as a Spiritual sense and in material prosperity.

Love with wisdom and starve from knowledge,[37] then you will see that you know your skills, successes, talents, and virtues in the abundance required to fulfill your life's purpose.

Energy is flowing freely through you, and it wants to materialize in superabundance. If you are not experiencing that flow of abundance then you have to ask yourself:

Why?

Is there something within me or around me that is blocking the abundant flow of prosperity?

Set your thoughts and frequencies on happiness and not on material wealth. Make sure your actions do not contradict your desires and that your actions mirror what you expect to receive from the Universe.

You must fully understand that you unconsciously attract what you think. When you truly love yourself in a "**deep profound love**", people will love you as well.

37 Meaning love from your own wisdom, not from worldly education.

You will bring more people, situations, and circumstances to you that reflect how you feel. What you attract will reflect how you truly feel at moments in either a negative or a positive environment. Do you really understand the implications of your state of being?

Learn to stay focused on the good side of yourself no matter what the outcome of the situation. Avoid those persons who oppose this positive way of thinking. They do so because of their own reasons and will do all they can to keep you off balance, set you in a negative state, or even try to erase your positive thoughts. You become a threat if the masses follow the "*Truth*."

Other hidden groups will disguise themselves and have high positions in government and religion. Religious fanatics will say you are following the Devil or whatever evil belief they have, in the name of their G—d. They will make you believe that to be saved you must believe in their fourteen hundred to two thousand year old faiths.[38]

Learn to love and respect yourself fully without being pretentious or acting conceited. When you truly love yourself, you will automatically be able to love others.

The only person who can make you truly happy is YOU. Only you are in charge of your happiness: not your parents, your children, partner, or anyone else. If you focus on complaints then that is what you will receive. Nobody can control your happiness; however, you have the opportunity to share it with everyone. Your joy lies within yourself.

When you think negatively, you are disconnecting yourself from the positive energy of the Universe. Negative thoughts are the cause of many of humanities' conflicts, illnesses, poverty, and unhappiness. So, once again say to yourself aloud; "*I AM THE BEST THERE IS.*

38 Refer to "Book III: Illuminatis The Ones and The Shadows"

I AM PERFECT IN EVERYWAY. I HAVE PERFECT THOUGHTS AND I ONLY SEE PERFECTION AND POSITIVE OUTCOMES IN MY LIFE".

Banish all negative, imperfect thoughts, and avoid people with negative energy including sources such as television or the internet. These negative messages do not serve you positively.

We have the misconception of what "*love*" is, as it is mostly understood in a physical sense. "*Love*" in its physical sense has been over—rated since in the Spiritual Realm it is not even close to how we perceive it.

Remember that you are the Master of your life and this includes your thoughts. The Universal Cosmic Consciousness[39] will answer your every command. If you see negative events, make light of them and then let them go. Put new thoughts of what you want in your mind. Feel them and be grateful for them. You must train your mind to see all the possibilities of what is around you with a positive outlook.

You were originally sent here for a purpose. You are here on "*vacation*" from a Spiritual Reality endowed with the wonderful power to shift, control, and, as a result, create your life. There are no limits to what you want or can receive because your ability to think is unlimited.

Everyone will create their own version of their vision so you cannot push your viewpoint onto them. Consider the fact that you can attract immense Universal forces when you believe a statement like "*Life was better years ago*" or "*The world has gotten more violent*".

39 The Universe exists as an interconnected network of consciousness, with each conscious being linked to every other. Sometimes this is conceived as forming a collective consciousness, which spans the Cosmos, other times it is conceived of as an Absolute or G—d head from which all conscious beings emanate.

I believe in sharing my well—being. I believe there is a superabundance of wealth for everyone to share. I believe in having loyal business partners, as in the round table. I believe you have the ability to choose what you really want to experience.

My mission is to empower and to share this with others, namely YOU. I plan to shape our wealth as one. This belief has always been around, even before time existed.

I have always been here. Only a few are aware of the reason and purpose?

Chapter 2

Surreptitious

"I much prefer the sharpest criticism of a single intelligent man to the thoughtless approval of the masses." — **Johann Kepler**

Prior to Creation, there was only the infinite filling all existence. Then IT arose to create worlds and emanate[40] the created. In the space of that void IT, emanated, created, formed, and made all the worlds.

I have mentioned this earlier but now let us present what was created and then hidden over sixty—five thousand years ago[41] and then re—discovered thirty—three hundred years ago. In spite of this, the fact that they were hidden and then found, the surreptitious[42] is now once again available to all of you who are willing to accept it. Only those in high positions and the few who discovered it knew about it over the years.

What is the restricted secret?

Why was it kept from being widely known?

40 This describes the first step in the process by which IT began.

41 Those who follow their religious beliefs assume the Earth is only eleven thousand years old.

42 Something kept from being noticed so that the general population would not receive the True knowledge. It was done in a concealed manner.

Who covertly operated this?[43]

What is this something that is being kept hidden from the masses?

Where did this begin?

When did this start?

How was this kept from you for so long?

The Truth is that this secret has always been in front of you, yet you chose not to see it. It is related to the Universe and how, with your mind, you can become one with its vibrating energy. Moreover, at the same time, this energy shapes your personality. Integrating this energy grants your wishes.

If you already know the secret to this mystery then this book, or any other similar book out there, is of no use to you.[44] Nevertheless, if you feel that you must learn it through reading books, please continue;[45] you shall acquire partial knowledge even though you will never attain the full Secret and its wisdom! Either you have the Gift and Power, or you just do not! There is no intermediate point.[46]

---

43 Not openly shown. Most of the answers shall be shown throughout this book.

44 Since visually this book seem to have the same concept, which you are right, if you read it like any other books.

45 You may know the basis of it. But the hidden codes have a much deeper meaning that is not as common as you may believe, but a surprising twist that is more powerful than any wealth you ever imagined. The Power is in the Hidden Codes throughout "The Universal Law of Creation" Chronicles.

46 You were told that we all have this gift, which is so far from the truth. The "Hidden Codes" are "specifically" for "each of you as individuals" and not for the mass general population to share with. A selective few will assume they know because of their "ego" and will lie to you with a false answer. The answer is a puzzle that each of you in secret and not publicly must combine as one.

A scribe is a person who writes books or documents by hand as a profession. However, before we had scribes, we did not "*write*" down our knowledge and history. We passed them down as "*words*" not to just anyone, but to those who have the gift to understand properly. For, if we were to write it, it would not be worth remembering since it could then be misinterpreted or miswritten.

Knowledge is gained through reading while wisdom is gained through experience. Both can be attained in the Spiritual Realm when you are called and you acknowledge it. It does not have to be a physical call. An experience you may have in the physical reality may seem just like a moment to you and everyone else. However, it is quite different while you are having a Spiritual experience, since it will seem only to "*you*" as more than one lifetime.[47]

When the time comes, when I will wonder what to say, or how to phrase it, I shall have my Higher Source work through me without hesitation. I will have another entity[48] represent me,[49] that which has the same connections, visions, and passions. I shall appoint this other as my spokesperson.[50] Through my Higher Source, I shall communicate from that moment on.

This secretive, clandestine knowledge lets you know that only you control how your life will go. It states that if you think positively about what you want in life, you shall have it just as you wished for it. The Surreptitious lets you know that only you control how life will develop. By consistently impressing your thoughts with this thinking, you can create that which you think is the meaning of the life you are living at this moment. This extends to your job, relationships, and all other

47 Refer to "Book II: Time is an Illusion"

48 A physical person.

49 Book III: Illuminatis The Ones and The Shadows Chapter 9: This is the Great Deception, subtitle "I The Greatest Error".

50 As in, the Biblical story of Moses who had his brother Aaron as his spoke person.

things around you. Your reality is strongly based on what you think and ultimately its changes on a constant basis.

You have the Power to Create your own reality of which "*only you notice*". Let me give you a simple example: You are crossing the street and you make a right turn, yet everyone else sees you going left.[51] People will see what they want to see since it is their illusion of what is happening to you. You can fall into their illusion of reality.

Before you "*Create*", you must "*Emanate*" it. When you are in doubt, now or later, you will not receive what you desired. Understand that time does not truly exist in the Spiritual Realm. Once you understand and comprehend this reality, and delete all present and future doubt, you shall receive your heart's desire. Like praying or wishing. However, the energy you are sending out is only floating around and it is not flying off to where you want it to reach. You are blocking it and do not even realize it.[52]

If part of the time you feel and think that you will become wealthy and successful, but the remaining time you are worrying about whether you really will be wealthy and be successful, you are sending out mixed messages to the Universe.[53] Do you follow? Yet, if you think that you "*are*" already wealthy and successful all the time, the Universe will see to it that you are "*within a position*" to make it into a reality.

You ask:

So now that I know, how do I correct my thoughts?

51 In Book II: "Time is an Illusion" I shall get deeper in this point.
52 For religious people: You are praying, however your prayer is floating around in the room you are in, and it is not floating up to where you want it to reach, as in Heaven.
53 Refer to Jake Hollow's "How to Deal with Emotions and the Life of a Motivational Speaker" Part II: Defining Emotion, Chapter 4: Anger, Fear, Stress, and Worry

You must intertwine yourself with the Universe. This means that you must become one with the Universe. For example if you want to buy a car, you must at least know what model you want, and its specific details. Now, what happens if you must have a car before the end of the month, but;

You are broke?

If you truly believe in this philosophy, and you intertwine yourself with the Universe using neutral—positive[54] thoughts and picture it without doubt, you "*will*" find the means to get that car by the end of the month. Positive or neutral thoughts bring positive things; negative thoughts bring negative things into your life. **FOCUS**!

You were born to be this person who you are, this you. Being realistic stops you from living out your dreams and from moving ahead. Learn to be unrealistic so that your dreams become reality. Always keep your eye on the prize and blinders around you to avoid distraction.

Once again, you are most likely looking over what I have written and will say to yourself;

What is the point, I am still broke, and I have no lover?

Now my two questions to you are;

Why is that?

Does poverty pull on you?

If you do nothing, you will reach poverty, do you follow? Therefore, to change this you have to focus on becoming prosperous both

54 Closer to positive energy over negative energy.

physically and Spiritually. You will attract the best in the crop as well as become rich and successful in all aspects of life if you apply this ancient philosophy.

You cannot achieve an understanding on how "*things*" work by studying dichotomies. It stands to reason, that you can become attractive by studying "*charisma*"[55] and "*charm*" or become wealthy by studying "*success*" and "*wealth*". You do not study their opposites… "*being unattractive*", "*being unloving*" or "*failure*" and "*poverty*," do you agree?

So if you think everyday that you will never have the kind of money you only dream of or that you shall never find the "*One*" in your life that will fulfill you, then read on.

In 1910, Wallace Delois Wattles[56] wrote that health, as a study of disease, would increase disease. Economics, as a study of poverty, would serve only to increase poverty. Consequently, you must focus your mind on prosperity— consciousness, in contrast to poverty—consciousness. So whatever you do, do not acknowledge failure as a bad thing; it is designed to be a stepping—stone to success. Do you follow?

Wattles also states in the first part of his book (of a three part series); "*The Science of Getting Rich*"[57] that you have a right to be rich. Furthermore, he also states that becoming so is a science, and not "*luck*".[58]

55 Remember that charisma is not something you are born with; it is something you develop.

56 He was an American author. A New Thought writer, he remains personally somewhat obscure, but his writing has been widely quoted and remains in print in the New Thought and self—help movements.

57 Wattles' other two books are "The Science of Being Well" and "The Science of Being Great"

58 Alternatively, fortuity is a belief in good or bad fortune in life caused by accident or chance, and attributed by some to reasons of faith or superstition, which happens beyond a person's control. "In my book "luck" is giving away your power."

He writes that there are two ways to become wealthy:

One is negative.

One is positive.

The negative way is through bidding "*competitively*" for wealth. Now, do not misunderstand this. By declaring this, he does not mean that competition, in general, is bad. Rather, he means that when you are aiming for something that exists in abundance, such as wealth, being competitive to an extreme is counter—productive. As a result, it has a multitude of negative processionary effects. You are only focused on your self—interest and not others.

The positive alternative is through creation.[59] When you become wealthy the "*creative*" way, you make it easier for others around you to become wealthy, as well. This also affects those who come after you.

He talks about the "*super wealthy*" becoming outdated.[60] As I mentioned before, he discusses how, in order to become wealthy, you must focus on prosperity and not poverty.

He has described many reasons why it is noble and honourable to pursue becoming wealthy via the "*creative*" method. He explains how you can only become all that you can be if you have enough money to clothe, educate, shelter, and develop, as well as nourish yourself more than just adequately. In order to satisfy these needs, you must become wealthy and doing this in a creative capacity is the honourable path. Do not be competitive. When you start doing good things naturally,

59 Refer to Jake Hollow's "How to Deal with Emotions and the Life of a Motivational Speaker" Part I: Life—Coaches on Internal Damage, Chapter 2: Challenge, subtitle "III Entrepreneur"

60 Read Wallace Delois Wattles books for more details.

when you no longer have to make an effort to do good things, then you will start to comprehend this philosophy.[61]

Wattles writes about "*use value*" and "*cash value*" and describes how you should always give more in "*use value*" than what you receive in "*cash value*". For example, if you have a painting that is valued at two thousand dollars, but you sell it to a person who has no appreciation for art at a much lower price, you have lost "*cash value*" in the process, am I not correct? (*Unless he/she is a dealer*).

Wattles also writes about how one must be willing to turn away "*any*" and "*all*" business that does not give customers more "*use value*" than the "*cash value*" they give you. He also says that because of this, the economy should be going into a slight deflation on a constant basis. He seems to have proven this repeatedly, even in today's market (*One hundred years later*).

People move away from the "*poverty mentality*" when they realize that they have a birthright to have and enjoy wealth, in general. This realization leads people to being generous. So, if you are positive and can use negative[62] to boost your confidence and self—esteem, then do so.

Every person who becomes rich by competition kicks down the ladder by which he rises and keeps others down. But, every person who gets rich by creation opens a way for thousands to follow him and inspires them to do so.

The middle class worships formal education because they understand it. It's linear. Creating wealth is non—linear by nature. If it offered a straight and narrow path to follow, there would be as many millionaires as there are college students. Seek formal education for

61 It will become second nature to do good things.
62 Transforming the negative into a positive.

the love of learning. Seek riches by teaching your self to think in non—conventional ways. The key to success, when small potential influences the larger scene, is to avoid pretentious ambitions and grandiose goals. The power of the small is served by slow and steady advancement, and succeeds through an honest awareness of its own limitations, without reservation.

You cannot get off the path you are on because the path isn't narrow, it is spherical; it includes the whole planet. Anywhere you put your foot is your path. Even the idea that you are not on the path is part of the path. Whatever is next for you, whatever you are struggling with right now is the key to your liberation. Don't resist your experience, whatever it is, embrace it.

If you're brave enough to risk, to temporarily live outside of your comfort zone, for a short period of time, you're big enough to win.

If you take time to ponder on what you want from life, you will discover the keys to achieving your hearts desire. Until then you are just being blown by the wind. You are a person who reacts instead of one who creates.

Those of you who truly lack,[63] or who are meek, do not need charity. What you require is "*inspiration*" and "*hope*." Charity only lasts for a moment while inspiration and hope will lead those of you in poverty to rise up to prosperity.

Those who have low self—esteem and confidence have lost their faith in life. Faith always starts with yourself; this means you must love yourself first, the Supreme Being next and then, finally, others. Once you fully understand and apply this, you will be able to afford to take

63 Meaning you are 'poor'.

risks causing dramatic changes in your life. You will recover faster, stronger, and smarter from every setback you will face.

If your job is "*structured*" and based on competition, then you are solely working for your own benefit on a commission basis, and not with your colleagues. In this situation, you are only thinking of yourself, and making your own sale. "*Creativity*", on the other hand, is more like you working as a team player and not solo, so that those who are your colleagues benefit with you. In this way you receive a team bonus pay, not a solo one.

This way you are:

Happy to help your colleagues' clients since it would not matter who writes the sale.

Working together instead of against each other in competition to achieve success.

I hope you see the advantage of a team bonus rather than an individual incentive.

Chapter 3

Positive Thought

"It takes but one positive thought when given a chance to survive and thrive to overpower an entire army of negative thoughts." — **Robert H. Schuller**

Whatever you choose to think will become your life experience. You have over sixty thousand thoughts a day. It is your job to keep so much information under control and keep it positive, by asking yourself everyday,

How do I FEEEEEL ?

Your frequency must be balanced[64] and in tune with the Universe. The "*Universal Law of Manifestation*" attracts a mirror that reflects your virtual reality. Therefore, by changing and charging your thought patterns, you can shift your vibration energy to whatever you want. Once you feel it deep inside, the Universe will change to your new strong vibrating feelings.

The "*Universal Law of Creation*" does not mix up its understanding of the frequencies it receives hence you must not violate this Ancient Law. It is certain and does so in obedience to the Law by which the Universe was created.

64 Neutral over Positive or Negative

The better you feel, the more you will attract things that help you feel good. Think hard and reflect your thoughts to this; it will make you become powerful on a higher degree of nobility, as well as more Cosmically aware. I strongly recommend that your own personal secret shifter be consistently on the neutral channel.

Some of you will say; "*Easier said than done. Moreover, I have been trying to change my reality. However, I'm not the only one doing that*".

Yes, I agree to this point. Now, let's go over each part of your comment; "*easier said than done*". Now analyze this saying and its belief.

This is a "*negative*" remark. You are focused on the negative and do not even realize it. Do you follow now?

To better understand "*frequency*," think of it as a wave of particular pitch or vibration that intervenes in space and/or time. Example: satellites in space, "*send*" pictures and sounds "*repeatedly*" with the hope that somebody like you out there will pick up the pictures, sounds, and watch television or listen to the radio.

You will create your own reality the moment you begin to fully understand and truly master your thoughts and feelings. You must be in tune with your inner—self, your outer physical self, as well as your Spiritual True—Self and sense where your freedom truly lies.

In addition to all that was mentioned before, you must know that within these three personas are where all of your Power is stored.

Remember, the Universe[65] is kind and not against you in any way.

65 It is neutral neither positive nor negative. It does not pick sides.

The most important question you can ask yourself has two parts:

Is this a friendly Universe?

Do I accept the Universe's friendliness?

Most people have been conditioned to believe that life is hard, but this is far from the truth! You were originally created to enjoy an abundant life. Then one day, our ancestors changed all that because of boredom and greed. Our government is doing the same thing to us, our children, our grandchildren, and generations that will come, blinding everyone more and more. I am here to wake you up to this awareness.[66]

So, release all your fears and doubts and scream to the Universe: "*LIFE IS EASY. IT IS SO GOOD THAT ALL GOOD THINGS COME TO ME! I DESERVE ALL GOOD THINGS; LIFE'S GOOD TO ME!*"

All good things are your birthright. YOU are the creator of yourself. Welcome to the magical you. YOU are your "*Lower*" or "*Higher*" self, both in the physical realm and the Spiritual Plain.[67]

You are made of energy, energy which is connected to the Universe.

How?

Thoughts are vibrating energy that are propelled throughout the Cosmos. It helps, and even warns, you who to trust and who not to. You must learn to sense and use negative energy and learn to transform it into a positive or neutral frequency. Example: Imagine that you hate your job and your life, so to change this you bring in neutral or positive

66 Refer to "Book III: Illuminatis The Ones and The Shadows" Chapter 11: The Dark / Light Universal Consciousness, subtitle "I BeginningEnd"
67 Refer to "Book II: Time is an Illusion"

subjection to your work environment. This at the same time will bring a smile to your face and improve your social life. If you cannot do this, I suggest you just walk away until whatever negative atmosphere around you is transformed into a positive.

Learning this concept leads to a fundamental change in behaviour. In other words, when you study a concept, you must learn to comprehend it and internalize it. By doing this, your perspective is no longer the same since through this process you have changed inside. You shall then conduct your life differently as a result, and align as well as intertwine yourself with your True Spiritual—Self.

All that you obtain in your life comes from your subconscious. It responds precisely to your thoughts. Your conscious mind affects your reality by sending your subconscious mind what you expect to manifest into your reality.

The Universe takes orders from your subconscious mind, so your subconscious belief is the "*key*". Therefore, if you surround yourself with negative thoughts, then negativity is what you will receive. Am I Correct? On the contrary, your desires will come to be when you condition your subconscious to surround itself with positive thoughts and get a firm idea about what you desire. Do this in conjunction with visualization in the physical world. By doing this, it "*will come*".[68]

You must know exactly the life you want, right here, right NOW. You just have to create your ideas as a three—dimensional reality with your thoughts and intentions.

Do not worry about how or when your desires will come to be, nor tell the Universe what to do or how to make it appear before you. Leave all those details to the Universe because it will not reach you a

68 The film "Field of Dreams" starring Kevin Costner

moment before or after you want it, but when you least expect it or even after you had forgotten all about it.

Therefore, when opportunity calls, just let it in and care for it with appreciation.

You are living the life you want at the present moment. You are living the reality your thoughts are reflecting. Therefore, if you feed your thoughts with negative energy, the Universe reads them that way and hence you attract your fears.

So once again, if you wish to change your life, you must change your way of thinking. Keep in mind that Moshe,[69] Y'shua,[70] Buddha,[71] Muhammad, and even Einstein and others like them, believed that if you should "*Ask*," and "*Believe*," you will "*Receive*".

All that you obtain in your life comes from your subconscious mind. It responds precisely to your thoughts.

Now, write down three questions about why you opened this book, or three situations you feel will help you by reading this book. Simply write three questions or situations that may help you in your life, your career, your relationship, or in what you want out of this.

69 Arabic as well as Hebrew for Moses.

70 Arabic as well as Hebrew for Joshua. This Y'shua full name would have been Y'shua ben Yosef (Joshua, the Son of Joseph), however Christians called him Jesus. Hebrew: Yehoshua; Greek: same as Jesus; Latin: Josue or Jesus in Hebrews; Arabic: Yusha' ibn Nūn. The first Joshua's name was Hoshea the son of Nun, of the tribe of Ephraim, but that Moses called him Joshua.

71 Hindustani pronunciation: meaning, "Awakened one" or "Enlightened One" in Sanskrit and Pali, in Devanagari script.

1. ______________________________

2. ______________________________

3. ______________________________

FOR THE MOMENT, DO NOT question why I am asking you to do this. I would just like you to trust me and yourself by doing this exercise.[72]

Ask and you shall receive. Unless you ask precisely for something that you want, you will receive differently. You must detach yourself from your fears, release them, and completely let go of what you think you want. You must then open yourself to infinite possibilities, no matter how you perceive them at first. Additionally you must be willing to change your situation instead of making excuses for it.

My assignment with this book is to help you to understand that you have to consistently and continuously ask the Universe for what you want in a humble manner.[73]

You must align, as well as intertwine, yourself with its energy source so that you can ask it anything and everything no matter what relative importance, or impact it has to you.

Write the statements I have asked you to or else please close this book since it will not help you, nor is it for you.

Why are you on this planet?

Why are we here in this existence?

72 From Jerry Maguire "Help Me, Help You!"
73 No hidden agenda.

Earlier, I wrote the answer that you are originally here, on vacation from the Spiritual Realm, to have a physical—matter life. This takes time and energy, you are here for a reason and a purpose; to experience helping yourself live out your dreams and affect the physical world around you.

You deserve this life, which is a privilege. Therefore, profit from this vacation and take advantage of it![74]

Life is often compared to a journey. Just as you may begin a trip with no final destination in mind, you could live your life without identifying its real purpose. If you do so, you are at risk of being caught up in what is called the "*business of life.*

Would you not agree that increasing your speed on a trip is pointless if you were not heading in the right direction?

Likewise, looking for meaning in life by simply improving your business will bring only emptiness, not True fulfillment.

The quest to understand why you are here transcends cultural and age differences. It stems from the profound requirement that you have a Spiritual side that can remain unsatisfied even after your material requirements have been met. Consider how some have worked to fill this "*need*" in their search for the purpose of life.

Many people associate success with the attainment of fame, fortune, or power. However;

Are these things the measure of real success?

74 Refer to "Book II: Time is an Illusion", it shall explain itself more on this subject

True success, at the very least, must be linked to sound ethical principles and a noble purpose in life.

What does it mean to you to be successful in life in general?

Society has made you believe that to succeed you must work harder and longer hours. This is nonsense.

You achieve more in less time when your personal and business time is balanced; when there is less conflict and stress.

Working hard has little to do with success; working smart with maximum effectiveness does, though. You must love your career and not treat it as a job, if not you are losing out. It is senseless to spend your time in something not personally rewarding and fulfilling. Do not take your career too seriously; make it fun.

You may believe that you must work long and hard to survive but this is a myth. You should work no more than thirty hours per week (*seven days*) and spend at least one day just focusing and thinking about better ways to live your life.

Do you believe that those who have amazing lives work more than they should?

Do you truly believe those who make more money than you work that much more than you do?

NO! Not at all. Those who have successful lives work less and think more. Life follows the same concept as business and relationships.

Less working hours plus more reflection time equals more wealth and satisfaction.

Money is called "*currency*" because it is used as a medium of exchanging energy from one entity to another. We will discuss how to use the Universal Law of Creation and how other Spiritual principles can be used to create a neutral or positive flow of currency/energy to you in order to manifest the things you want in life.

You see, these people take the time to think, dream, and make their wishes happen. They are passionately hungry to secure a better, more exciting life than the rest of the world. They picture it clearly in their mind and hold on to that image steadily until it becomes a definite thought form. It is all up to you to see this. You have to know what life you want, right here, and demand that life **NOW**.

So which one are you?

Do you "call for" the life you want?

Do you "call for" who you want to be, right here, right now?

Do you demand that life?

You have to live for that life **NOW**.

Seeing life in a different perspective changes how you live because of how you conceptualize it. To illustrate let me present these examples;

Is it more difficult for you to make ten thousand dollars in less than a year (*365 days*) or for you to have the girl/boy next door as a girl/ boyfriend?[75]

Think consciously on this question before you answer it and then read the next paragraph.

75 Your answer would most likely be "Yes, no problem"

Is it more difficult for you to make one million dollars or for you to have Miss America/Mister Universe or a World Supermodel as your girl/boyfriend?[76]

The only difference between these two statements is in how you look at them as being too hard or impossible.[77]

For example, if you were to travel from Montréal to Florida by car or from Montréal to Rome (*Italy*) by plane;

What route would be longer?

What route would take more time?

Once again, think consciously on these questions. Only you can control what makes your life easier or harder. Only you can look at an "*obstacle*" as a problem or a solution. Life works on your own logic and belief.

In your dreams, you must be specific about the nature of all of your wishes and desires. As I have stated before, when you want to buy a new car or meet a beautiful woman/man you must consider all possible details of these desires:

What kind of car do you want?

What price are you willing to spend?

What color do you want?

76 So, if it was "Yes" for the other, then it should also be possible for this. See also Chapter 7: The Start of the Calling

77 Most of you see the first two question as possible, and the other two question as a "maybe" or not possible.

What make?

What year?

What model?

What options?

What kind of character and personality do you desire from the opposite sex?

What nationality should she/he be?

What hair color and length?

What body type?

What age?

What background?

What other important qualities?

Your mind gets confused with the options and loses direction if you are not focused.

Chapter 4

Envisioning Your Ideas to Reality

Trance tips

"First comes thought; then organization of that thought, into ideas and plans; then transformation of those plans into reality. The beginning, as you will observe, is in your imagination." — **Napoleon Hill**

Here are some exercises on self—help trances that you can do by yourself or with another person softly whispering to you:

Relax, close your eyes; do not squeeze your eyelids too tightly.

Put your hands on your sides loosely, your feet on the floor. Remain calm.

Repeat each definition three times then pause after each word. Create an intense mental image in your subconscious.

Visualize that "*my car is beautiful!*" Make this a part of your reality. Visualize this in vivid detail; "*My car is beautiful! My car is beautiful!*

My car is beautiful!" Visualize a brighter future. Make this a part of your reality.

Visualize, in vivid detail, the brighter future you desire. "*My car is beautiful! My car is beautiful! My car is beautiful!*" You can do this even in a noisy environment; you are not forced to be in a quiet area.

Relax, close your eyes; do not squeeze your eyelids too tightly.

Put your hands on your sides loosely, your feet on the floor. Remain calm.

Repeat each definition three times then pause after each word. Create an intense mental image in your subconscious.

Visualize that "*She/he is all over me.*" Make this a part of your reality. Visualize this in vivid detail; "*She/he is all over me right now! She/he is all over me right now! She/he is all over me right now!*" Visualize a brighter future. Make this a part of your reality.

Visualize, in vivid detail, the brighter future you desire. "*She/he is all over me right now! She/he is all over me right now! She/he is all over me right now!*" You can do this even in a noisy environment; you are not forced to be in a quiet area.

This is just a baseline; the rest is up to you to add on what you desire. You should change the "*quotes*" to suit your desires by writing a minimum of ten different options to fit your desires. Once you have done so, read them twice a day. This should be done before you go to sleep and when you wake up.[78]

78 Before you open your eyes or yawn.

When you are meditating or in a trance state, the position is not essential.[79] What is important is for you to be fully comfortable, so you can sit, lie down, stand up, or whatever is most comfortable for you. What is significant is your breathing, which you should focus on, that fills your lungs.

Having Spiritual music around you is good; it will relax and help make you powerful. It will help your creativity, and put you in tune with the Universe. Being in yourself does not help, but being in your Spirit does change you. Pride, arrogance, conceit, and deceit are enemies that can destroy you. It is better to be humble and strong.

Bring to mind that the "*Clandestine Creation*" is the Secret of the Universe.

How you deal with life, in general, is how you perceive it to be, while you, on the other hand, create your own reality of success. Otherwise, you now consciously control your conscious, not the subconscious controlling you.

Now back to a trance state.

Meditation or Meditating—into—a Trance can be better accomplished by not cutting your hair on any part of your body. I know this seems crazy. However, if you want to achieve the best results, then do not cut what we were created with and that grows naturally. You do not have to agree because you have become accustomed to the Twenty—First century style of living which is to be shaven and clean—cut. Yet, if it grows, there must be a reason for none of your physical characteristics were given to you without reason. By respecting the creation, you respect the creator.

79 Roman Brave would disagree with this

If you do this exercise with another person, then one person should be behind you facing the same way, while you are comfortably sitting in a chair. That person should rub your temple and move all their energy to their fingers tips and vibrate them down from your head to your lower back, while you are "*in trance*", and they should whisper to you, in a calm voice, the suggestions I have just written for you. This is called **TRANCE.**

Wake up, open your eyes, and then focus on a new thought:

> *"Deep down in my heart I truly believe, without any shadow—of—a—doubt whatsoever that… I am happy, grateful, stronger, and can live out my dreams…NOW!"*

Whatever you do, do not obsess over the ideas you focus on during trance. The reasons for this will be explained later on.

Lead yourself into trance with the steps presented previously just before you go to sleep and when you wake up. Continue by adding more dreams to personalize the experience, both in the professional and personal sides.

Go ahead and do it now! Do this to help motive yourself to stay positive; by visualizing your dreams, wishes, and desires, you can create positive energy, emotions, and feelings about them.

In your mind, sense, see, touch, taste, feel, believe, and live the experiences. These are your visions and dreams, wishes and desires and you will be excited about them. Visualizing your dreams and wishes with positive energy, emotions, and enthusiasm is one of the best ways to eliminate doubt.

Do not let negative thoughts and emotions enter your mind or visions. With the aid of positive feelings of accomplishment and excitement, you can leave feelings of doubt and inadequacy on the back burner. No, you are not just faking it, you are envisioning!

Your mind never sleeps; your subconscious mind is always working. Your subconscious mind sparks your ability to transform what you think into reality. That is why the best time to visualize your wishes is when you are going to sleep and once you wake up. Keep the list I have asked you to write next to you so that you can review it before you turn off the lights; then start your trance and meditation. Visualize the realization of your wishes.

You must not only believe that it "*will*" happen, but that it "*did*" and "*has*" already happened. You must believe in what you "*want*" or "*wish*", that it… "*IS*"!

During your hours of sleep, your subconscious will continue on its own. It will organize, explore options, and come up with solutions and paths to solve them. By doing this, you are controlling your subconscious and making it work overtime for you.

Remember that the answers will not appear immediately upon awakening. It is like building your muscles, this takes time.[80] Do not expect to get into physical shape in one day, do not expect to look in the mirror, flex your arms, and as a result see yourself with a great body. Building physical muscles is a gradual process that requires you to be patient and realistic about seeing progress.

However, you must act as "*if*" you had it **NOW**. When you force that belief, the result comes faster. For instance, if you talk to your friends about being broke and not being able to take someone out on a "*date*", but at the same time, you say you want to date, you are

80 Same concept on losing weight

contradicting yourself. Change it by saying "*I can take someone out on a date. I can afford it.*"

If you are a writer, and your books talk about how women/men[81] leave their partners or you are just writing a fictional book where, on the cover, women/men have their backs turned away from the readers.

What does this imply?

You are writing about failed relationships and the book cover represents that women/men are not interested in you.

The problem is you want to date, this is what "*you*" say in private, yet your inner most thoughts do not reflect that in your books or on each cover you have illustrated.[82] Do you follow?

By deliberately choosing to change your writing and book covers to reflect what you want, there will be no contradiction in your desire. With this, you will see a proven difference.

Learning this new skill of trancing, at first, may make you feel stupid, uncoordinated, and even angry. You may feel like a real klutz. You might feel weird and awkward but do not let that stray you away from your objective. Stay focused, not because you have to, but because you want to. One day, you will say, "*I'm glad I committed to it.*"

Stare at your ceiling while you do this and do not make excuses for not doing it. Always visualize in the present tense. Do not use the past or future tense because yesterday is already gone and tomorrow might never come. See yourself in your dreams and wishes as if you

81 Male or female writer (depending on which sex you are interested in).

82 Even the paintings you have on your walls, books or magazine you read, movies or television programs you watch, and the list goes on.

are already where you want to be. Compress time to the now, at your present moment.

Remember, everything that has been created was once a vision. All was a vision before it became a physical reality.[83] Once you get into the "habit" of constantly visualizing the results you want, they will become real. You will notice an increase in your self—confidence and your level of enthusiasm. You will identify the point previously explained where your visions become the experiences of your present life. Once you can visualize your wishes and dreams, you will accomplish them. Intertwining yourself with the Universe is your goal.

When trancing, do not underestimate the importance of values. It is essential to ask yourself:

Am I designing my life around that which I value most?

Is what I am working to achieve something I truly value?

Am I experiencing any conflict between my goals, dreams, wishes, desires, and my values?

Have my accomplishments or failures produced empty or exciting feelings?

When you are visualizing, be careful to avoid any negative information. Block out those negative thoughts with positive visions. Train yourself. Train yourself. Train yourself. I cannot emphasis this more. Train yourself to the fullest.

Another tool you can use is Meditation. This must be explained as being different from a Trance. You can do this exercise on your own or

83 Flying in a plane, going to the moon, was once a "unrealistic" dream.

with others; however, you cannot interfere with the practice of others around you.

I will show you how to learn the Universal Law of Creation. Pretend that you are Aladdin.[84] In this analogy, the Secret is the lamp, while the Genie represents the Universal Consciousness, which is the Universal Law of Creation.

The Universal Law of Creation will give you everything you want since you are the Master. Now, you must follow three steps[85] While you image you are floating in space and being one with the Universe. Do the following!

ASK: *Give the Universe a command!* Write it down on a piece of paper. Ask the Universe what you want, what you require, and work out your desires in detail in order to avoid giving the Universe mixed messages.

The Universe (warehouse) might see your message as a negative signal and not a positive one. Remember this may happen even if it was not your intention to do so.

Look at the Universal Consciousness as a catalogue and choose from it your desires in the same way you place an order in the internet. When you order from a catalogue or a website, you have to wait until your order is delivered but you know you have it even if it is not in your hands yet.

BELIEVE: *You must believe what you commanded is already yours.* You must believe that you have already received it. See the things you want as if they were already yours and believe it unconditionally. You

84 An Anglicisation of the Arabic name 'Alā' ad—Dīn, Arabic: عالء الدين literally "nobility of the faith."
85 As in three wishes

must ask, speak, and think in the present that you have it and received it. Do not doubt it otherwise you will not receive it. The Universe will accommodate events so that you can receive it. You must convince yourself that you already have it before you actually do. Claim the things you want and all obstacles will move out of your way. Make believe until it becomes real.

RECEIVE: *Feel it now and feel good so the Universe and your desire know you want it, and it "IS"*. You are required to feel it. Put your frequency on all good things to come. You will receive all of the things that make you feel good. You will receive all good things now. You know, you feel, and you create. Life is what you make it.

Ask, **Believe**, and **Receive**.

Once you bring even a small doubt into this, the Universal Consciousness will knock out what you should have received and send you what you did not want, so you will have to re—start all over again.

You have come to an age where you must develop your own personal belief and not rely on what your parents believed. The Universal Consciousness is real; you can use valid objects to examine it. It is in your nature to examine the Universe to comprehend it. That is, it follows certain laws and is predictable. However; most of us are poor examiners.

Usually we are subject to prejudice, and we have a profound tendency "*to see what we want to see rather than what is really there*". Consequently, to examine it, and hence understand accurately, it is necessary for you to put yourself through the discipline of experience, so that you cannot feel that you know something unless you have actually experienced it.

While the discipline method begins with experience, a simple experience itself is not to be trusted. Experience must be repeatable, usually in the form of an experiment. Along with the event, the experience must be verifiable, and in that, others must have the same experience under the same circumstances. You no longer go by blind faith.

This may seem strange, but not only should you change outside, but also inside. Even if you are in the same old place, change how you see it. The whole world desires to look different, feel different. Feel how warm, safe, loving, exciting, and good it is for you are a part of the solution.

Possibilities are endless. Because you are now open to suggestion and optimistic about the future, you are apt to interact with great people. Consciously determined work and energy will create positive results.

Chapter 5

Humble

"Keep your thoughts positive, because your thoughts become your words.
Keep your words positive, because your words become your behaviour.
Keep your behaviour positive, because your behaviour becomes your habit.
Keep your habits positive, because your habits become your values.
Keep your values positive because your values become your destiny."
— **Mahatma Gandhi**

The negative force only comes inside you when you let it. So every time you blame it, it becomes stronger in you. You give it power.

When what I could perceive as "*a bad thing*" happens to me, I just ignore it as if it was not there and I move on. The "*bad thing*" gives up.

It looks for other weaknesses, nonetheless. For example, it can come in many forms such as jealousy of others doing "*seemingly*" better than you. You saw through it and made sure it did not distract you because as soon as you feel the jealously creep in, you will understand that this is a negative force that is affecting you.[86] This is what makes you stronger.

86 You are as the mass population that lets your negative emotions control you. By realizing this, you have the choice to let it win or not

Certain trains of thought are unhealthy, and you know this, though it is hard to stop yourself. Do not try, but do it. If you have the discipline to break one thought chain, you have the power to create your life.

The way the Universe is designed, it is all just waiting for that insignificant little spark from your hearts to set all the beauty and Truth in motion. It is so unimaginably perfect.

Become humble[87] and once you recognize who you really are and become enlightened, you will suddenly have access to all the Power in the Universe. I believe that knowing where you are going really helps, and that constructive change begins when you are finally able to say; "*I'm really ready*".

If you have faith, you can move mountains from one area to another. Ask it to move from here to there, and it will move; nothing will be impossible for you if you absolutely believe it with no doubt. Trancing, meditating, praying, fasting[88] and intertwining yourself with absolutely no shadow—of—a—doubt whatsoever, will make it… happen.

You must believe and convince yourself of this. Assuredly, not only must you have faith, you must without doubt. Even the existence of the dust of one particle of the intention that you shall accomplish what you ask, and you shall not… creates your desire.

If you should ask the mountains to now cast themselves into the sea, it will be done. Whatever you ask for by praying and believing, you will be receiving it.

87 Read Book III: Illuminatis The Ones and The Shadows Chapter 9: This is the Great Deception, subtitle "I The Greatest Error"

88 Abstention from food minimum one day maximum forty days.

If you believe, all things are possible. Have faith and intertwine yourself with the Universe and see yourself as one with the Universe. You must have absolutely no shadow—of—a—doubt whatsoever in your heart, but you must believe that the things you ask for will be done. All things you ask for and believe that you have already received, as a result will, happen.

Once you question it… POOF! It will disappear or be taken away from you, before it even reaches you.

Be persistent when you ask, and believe in it until you receive it.[89] For it will be given to you. Seek and you will find it. The Universe will open its door if you knock on it hard enough.

Ask

Believe

Receive

There are certain things in life you cannot explain in words. For instance, if you have never tasted ice cream, no matter how hard I explain the taste to you, you will not understand it until you personally dip into ice cream yourself. Do you follow? Hence, I can say, I have always been here, and only a selected few shall understand that.

To draw towards you the realization and manifestation of your desires, you must first be clear and be fully aware of what those desires truly are.

89 Without dwelling on it

As I have been asking of you throughout my book, please pick up a pen and paper or any electronic device where you can make yourself a list and then describe your desires on:

Career

Children

Finances

Health

Hobbies

Home

Pets

Relationships

Spirituality

Travel

You do not have to limit the list to these areas of your life; you can extend to it to all that is important to you. It is whatever you truly desire in your life. This list will become the focus of your highest aspirations.

For this reason, do not set limits to your imagination, for it is the "*Universal Foundation of Plenty*", this is just fulfilling your requirements, not inflating your human ego—self. Ask only for the things you really require to fulfill your life's purpose.

Why?

Could it be that you are not successful in Spirituality, hence, there is no balance in your life. Do you follow?

Now pause and figure out what this means on your own, without any help.

When practicing the keys to abundance, you are working with the "*Laws of Energy*", and you are fully responsible for its "*use*" or "*abuse*". In the same way abundance is created, you can create a negative vibration if you use the energy at your disposal to create things that you do not require, such as selfishness.

Whatever you truly desire, **WILL** "*eventually*" come to you. You draw it to yourself, therefore take the time to question your motives and evaluate your desires.

Always picture something better than the best of what you are experiencing now. You always want to be reaching for something higher.

As you know, in the physical reality, you never get something for nothing. "*The Universal Law of Creation*" is clear on this. When you give to life, you receive from life. Therefore, if you stop giving yourself to the world, you will stop receiving from it.

If you have a one—track mind, you limit your options. When you are overly attached to or anxious about something, you are not open to the surprise packages or new opportunities that may be right in front of you. You blind yourself.

Take the necessary steps to get the momentum started. You get what you want out of life as long as you really want it and are committed to getting it.

The flow of Spiritual and material abundance is often good; bad things, however, because of the negative blockages, can happen and may compete with what your desire. You may want to go in a certain direction, but your vibration takes you off the beaten track of your mission. Do not fight it, let it lead you. Dealing with your Spiritual vibration should be your first priority.

Each day, a new parcel of the negative energy you have created in your present life, and past lives, is delivered to your front entrance for resolution. You may experience that energy as the breakdown of your health, your finances, relationship, or just the breakdown of your car. Things just do not seem to move the way they should. Do you follow?

I don't live by other people's expectation of who I should be, or act as. What is amazing is when I find that someone else wrote what I felt was originally my thoughts and writings years before me. That confirms how connected I am instead of being separated as I used to believe. When I quote someone's word, I give them the full credit. I feel not alone as I used too, but that we are connected in synchronicity.

All my life I felt alone and kept everything to myself, until I was incarcerated which helped a lot. I've learnt to rely on "*logic*" instead of "*emotion*". I just write about my personal experiences and in what I know, and leave as it.

Telling me or suggesting how I should be is not your place. How you in vision a "*Shaman*", a "*Guru*", a "*Spiritual Teacher*" and so on is not reality, but a conception that you believe it is.

I. Prosperity is Abundance

THE DIVINE DISTRIBUTION OF WEALTH on this physical plane occurs according to the energy patterns and Spiritual law. In most cases, every person who has joy, love, money, and all good things, is entitled to it according to their vibration. This is the case even if they did not earn it in one lifetime, but may have received it through inheritance or lottery.

Joy, love, money and more comes to you because there is something in the Etheric[90] (*or Causal*) Body that attracts wealth to their being. It may also be written into their blueprint (or Life Chart) for whatever karmic[91] purpose.

When you practice the "*Laws of Abundance*" you create good energy, and therefore, you begin to attract prosperity to yourself.

The possession of joy, love, money and all the rest does not make a person better or worse. Joy, love, money and all good things are a responsibility. A form of prosperity is having a great deal of joy, love, and money that should not be dammed, as this will block the flow.

The secret to prosperity is to give. Another is to use your gifts and talents. By wisely using your gift, you triplicate them.

This is not only related to a financial side. Monetary currency is merely a medium of exchange.

90 Represent one of the planes of existence. It represents the fourth [higher] subplane of the physical plane (a hyperplane), the lower three being the states of solid, liquid, and gaseous matter.
91 The force generated by a person's actions to perpetuate transmigration and in its ethical consequences to determine the nature of the person's next existence.

This concept can also involve:

Services

Things you do for others

It can involve other people as well as your immediate and extended family

Another secret to prosperity is to stop looking to other people for your supply. Look to the Universe; do not depend upon any human being.

Always keep a "*seed*" of prosperity and keep your thoughts uplifted.

No matter how poor you are, always keep a few hundred dollars somewhere that you call 'fall back on' money. You do not have to keep a lot, but always keep at least a few hundred dollars in cash tucked away somewhere.

This is the seed for prosperity.

If you learn not to let go of every cent, but to hang on to enough to tide you over, you will have confidence in that seed. Then you can apply to the Universe. In reply, it will provide you with the wisdom to transform what you have in order to receive more. However, if you spend everything you have, then your confidence (*and faith*) will be shaken.

So keep a seed of prosperity, and keep your thoughts in a very positive state. Your thoughts have a great deal to do with your prosperity.

Sometimes the way to break a pattern is to actually spend money.

The reason why prosperity does not flow into your life is that you have stopped giving. Another secret of prosperity is that you have to release something from yourself, as you may be stifling the flow.

You must understand how to work with the "*Laws of Abundance*". You work with them through affirmations, meditation, trance, prayer, and neutral or positive thinking. Additionally, by ensuring that the "*Law of Stagnation*" does not function in your life, you must avoid the damming up of your supply.

To tap into the flow of prosperity, everyone should develop their faith in the "*Universal Law of Creation*", and know that your requirements will be taken care of, no matter what they are.

It is '*negative*' to worry about your future. This can, in fact, dam up the flow of prosperity into your life. The moment you start worrying, you tune into the millions of people who are worrying, as well.

You may not be aware of it, but their thoughts and energies will be attracted like a magnet into your subconscious, your thought patterns, and your daily life. This leads to a downward spiral.

One of the greatest secrets of prosperity is to tune into 'right thinking,'[92] by thinking "right".

Learn to develop the belief that no matter what you require, it will be supplied to you.

In order for the "*Law of Abundance*" to truly be activated, you must also be aware of the other Spiritual Laws.

92 Neutral or positive thinking

Chapter 6

Cause of Tension

"For those who believe, no proof is necessary. For those who don't believe, no proof is possible." — **Stuart Chase**

Money is called "*currency*" because it is used as a medium of exchanging energy from one entity to another. We will discuss how to use the Universal Law of Creation and other Spiritual principles to create a positive flow of currency/energy to you in order to manifest the things you want in life.

You have to realize that money really controls humans now. Money is good if the energy flows with good intention. However, it can lead to wars when people get greedy.

High ranking people in the military, scientists, and world leaders know just what is going to happen in the near future. It is mostly the ordinary people who are still in a sleep.

They think that it is made up and nonsense.[93] Everyone works as usual and lives their lives. Most are unaware of what is happening behind the scenes. When the curtain is opened, a shock might easily

93 That they are being enslaved. Deeper explanations shall be revealed in Book III: Illuminatis The Ones and The Shadows.

occur. Then we suggest that you take a deep breath. It is not to question them; it is about being big enough to take responsibility for our planet and ourselves.

If you are a nail biter to the point of going down to your skin, this is a clue that you are nervous and unsure of yourself. In addition, you certainly lack some confidence.

The trick to stop biting your nails is not to focus on not biting, since the more you are thinking of not biting, the more you will want to bite them.

The best advice I can give you is this; "*you must be focused on lifting your self—esteem*". Once you build up your confidence, along with stopping all your worries, you will then notice that you unconsciously are no longer biting your nails. Only you control who you are, what you do, as well as what you want to be.

On trance or meditation techniques, you might feel dizzy, stoned, light—headed, see colours, and lights etcetera. Remember, you are doing this to gain control, not to get a rush. Keep your back straight, eyes closed; listen to transcendental music and keep your mind focused. Fears and worries have no place in this, so whenever one comes up, stay calm, just watch it come and let it go. Do not get sucked into this negative vibe even for a moment. Keep complimenting yourself with your wishes. There are times when Higher Forces take over, when physical laws simply do not apply. Trust yourself, and trust your inner guide as you tune into your connection with the Power of the Universe.

First, learn to be more objective about things that makes you angry or jealous. If you can just quiet down a minute and "*feel*" what's going on in your heart and mind, you can learn to work with it in a better way than slamming your fist through the wall or biting your nails to the bone.

You can get more on these details from Steve Piccus and Roman Brave. Steve is a Master in trance, while Roman is quite good in meditation. If you decide to carry out these practices, take a vow to do it every day for a minimum of one month before you decide whether it suits you or not. Yoda, the Jedi Master on Star Wars said, "*Do or do not... there is no try*".[94] I say; "*You do not try, you do it or you don't.*" Do not "*try*" it once or twice, than get "*lazy*", and give excuses why you stopped.

Do not do it because you want it quick and on fire at that moment. Bear in mind that when the flames die down, you find an excuse.

Trance, meditation, and intertwining yourself with the Universe is an Ancient technique. Most of the change in your life has been on the surface. If you want to go for a deeper change, you have to be willing to be patient. Your mind will give any excuse to reduce the intensity of your daily Spiritual practices.

You picked up my book because you believed you were searching for help, am I right? Maybe that was not the true reason. Maybe you felt a Spiritual "*calling*". However, if you just picked it up out of curiosity, but not because you believe in Spiritual Gurus, then once again I would have to ask you to please put this book down now, and pass it on to someone who does want it, for they sense the "*calling*".

If you are a hopelessly negative person who acts secure but is secretly weak and not connected to this incredible beautiful world, lying to yourself all is your choice but don't take it away from those who held this in their immense hearts.

94 Try = Lazy.

The first key to unblocking yourself is:

> *Be* **GRATEFUL** *for everything that happens to you including the good or bad.*

Be grateful for the joy and beauty of all creation, including the beauty of your own soul. Be continuously grateful for all that you are and what you have, and you will see how your abundance increases.

Be grateful for everything that happens to you. Count the negatives, the positives, the miracles, the disasters — everything — because they are teachers teaching you your lessons.

Even when things are not going as you would like, be grateful for being shown that there are some adjustments you must make in order to make things right.

In negative situations, when you find it difficult to be grateful, it is important to realize that anything coming towards you is energy arriving. Bless the messenger who delivers that particular bundle of energy then reclaim and transmute it into something positive.

Be grateful and see the light in everyone you meet. There is something special about everyone and you can help them see what it is.

I. You Made Yourself

Do not ever think, in a selfish way, that you are better than who you really are. Do it only if it helps others improve their lives. Use your good sense and measure yourself by the amount of faith and belief you have.

Your body is made up of many parts. In addition, each of them has its own use, do you agree? You, me, along with everyone else, are the same with the Universe. We are many, yet we are each a part of the Universe, the Divine Being. You are part of the Universal Body, as well as part of every living entity. You are all intertwined with others. You are all connected; you are all Spiritual Beings, energy fields operating in a larger energy field.

Energy cannot be created nor destroyed, however it does change forms. Energy can take different forms and is a living entity. This energy determines whatever you may be thinking and feeling. Everything you want is made of energy which means it vibrates. By practising when we are young, we learn to move, do you agree? Now by connecting and intertwining yourself with the Universe, you can do the same with the energy of our thoughts.

When you are sending a vibration into the Universe, at the frequency of your energy, the Universe receives your signal and gives back what you want from its invisible vibration data collective warehouse. Therefore, if you send the Universe a negative vibrational energy frequency, you shall receive negative things in return. On the other hand, if you send the opposite you will receive what you really want. I do hope you follow me now.

Those of you who are a part of the "*Ones*" or the "*Shadows*"[95] have been given different gifts to use. Each of you are at a different level. If you can prophesize, you should do so according to the amount of belief or faith you have. If you can serve others, you should serve. If you can teach, you should teach. If you can encourage others, you should encourage them. If you can give, you should be generous. If you are a natural leader, you should "*do*" your best to lead, not "*try*". If you are good to others, you should do it cheerfully.

Be sincere in your love and have gratitude for others; hold on tight to everything that is good. Honour others more than you do yourself. Never, ever give up. Let your hope and your belief make you happy and grateful.

Be patient in times of trouble; in addition, never stop writing down your wishes.[96] When you see others truly happy, be happy with them so you can feed off of their positive energy. Be friendly with everyone but do not let anyone take you for granted. Do not act proud nor feel that you are smarter than those around you.

Make friends with ordinary people and teach them that they can be, or have, whatever they want if they truly believe. Do not mistreat this gift nor mistreat those who may have mistreated you; just walk away. Do not try but earn the respect of others, in addition, do your best to live peacefully with everyone.

Do not get even with the people who hurt or betray you. Their negative waves will be returned back to them three fold when it should be, and not one minute before you want it to happen or a minute after you want it. Your best revenge, as Steve Piccus (stevepiccus.com) said

95 Explanations shall be revealed later on in Book II: Time is an Illusion and Book III: Illuminatis The Ones and The Shadows.
96 Not "wishes" that it will be? But "wish" that it "IS" here already.

to me was "*that you become physically healthier, financially wealthy, and patient*". This is not a myth, but a fact.

Live your life like in your dreams, but do not over drink to get drunk or be vulgar, for you will turn your dreams into your nightmares. You are a Powerful Energy in a physical body, a Spirit in the flesh, Eternal Life expressing itself, a Cosmic Being; you are all wisdom, intelligence, perfection, magnificence. Moreover, you are a Creator.

Say this aloud; "*I'M IN CONTROL. I'M THE MASTER OF ME. I'M GREATNESS. I'M WHAT I WANT TO BE!*"

If your actions do not cause doubts, you are fortunate. But, if you do have doubts, you are going against your beliefs. You know that whatever you are doing is wrong, so follow your beliefs. Always follow your gut; always follow your first instincts.

Blessing people and their home is an amazing thing in today's age. You do not have to be in a religious belief to believe in being blessed. Times have changed; now people are embracing alternate Spiritualities. I have the gift of conducting such ceremonies. This has nothing to do with religious practices but is a Twenty—First century new way of connecting yourself with your Spirituality. It is a way to deal with both the physical and emotional aspects of transition. Most want these blessings when negative things happen to them while others keep having positive things in their life and stay fresh. People do it once to twice a year to clear their old energy with a newer and stronger positive one.

I[97] can help you with this but you must work with me to make it happen. Do not take this blessing for granted as you will turn it into a

97 Sometimes the *"I"*s is referring to my Higher—Self or through the guide of my Spiritual Guide.

curse. You will definitely get a sense of inviting some positive Spiritual energy into yourself or home.

I believe in group participation as long as everyone has an open, positive mind energy around them and are all attuned to each. I will light a candle for each individual, have him or her blessed, and ask for his or her wishes with mine.

This practice has been around for thousands of years but most people have forgotten about it or do not know how to ask for it. It is a lack of awareness, for people confuse religion for Spiritual belief. This ritual itself is important because of the benefits it promises to generate. This, I believe, is vital in your life and will help the void for those who are not religious or who are atheists.

I happen to believe that you can feel a positive energy and a psychological benefit after a blessing. All I ask is;

What kind of blessing do you want (in details)?

What do you want to happen that will help you smile?

You may conscientiously practice the keys to abundance, yet still you do not achieve the results you desire. This is because you have not cleared your subconscious from useless ideas.

You may decide to start affirming,

I AM SUCCESSFUL …

However, if you have been telling yourself for the last few years[98] that you are a failure, your subconscious mind is not going to be too easily convinced.

Your subconscious is like a recording machine. It records every impression you have absorbed throughout your life.[99] That includes all the negatives you have heard and believed about yourself.

Every time you think something negative about yourself, every time someone criticizes you or intimidates you, your subconscious mind records the event.

Often you do not realize just how much you have been influenced by another's thoughts or words. These negatives can undermine your abundance.

In the highest dimensions of Spirit, your soul knows no boundaries and it wants to be liberated from the domination of negative subconscious programming. The subconscious not only records negative impressions, but it replays them just like a tape recorder on automatic replay; it plays back the recordings of the past.

You must re—program your subconscious with neutral—positive messages. This is what positive affirmations are all about: affirming the innate beauty and positive potential of the soul.

Another key for working with your subconscious is to ask your divine self to take dominion over the four components of the mind:

The subconscious mind.

98 Or a few lifetimes.
99 And your past lives.

The conscious mind.

The unconscious mind.

The Superconscious mind.

By doing this you seal your subconscious so it does not become a tyrant over your soul. You also empower your divine self to generate neutral—positive energies and impulses in the subconscious and unconscious.

The Superconscious mind is the mind of Infinite intelligence that works through your highest self.

The conscious mind is the reasoning mind.

On a Spiritual level, the subconscious mind corresponds to your desires, and this is why it is so influential. When the subconscious mind is cleared and functioning in a healthy way, the subconscious acts like a resilient trampoline, catapulting your highest aspirations into action.

The unconscious mind is the deepest level of your being and can exercise great power over you although it is not directly accessible from your awareness.

When you begin to work on your subconscious mind, do not be too surprised if you see the negatives coming up more intensely and with more frequency. The more faith, determination, and joy you have, the more Spiritual light will naturally expose the blocks to your Spiritual progress.

Chapter 7

The Start Of The Calling

"Interdependence is and ought to be as much the ideal of man as self—sufficiency. Man is a social being. Without interrelation with society, he cannot realize his oneness with the universe or suppress his egotism. His social interdependence enables him to test his faith and to prove himself on the touchstone of reality." — **Mahatma Gandhi**

When I talk about the Spiritual Realm,[100] I am not talking about any physical desire. I am talking about our True Spiritual thoughts in the Spiritual Realm that has plans and does not interfere with our physical dilemma because the True Higher You picked the physical life you are living to acquire knowledge.[101]

My primary aim is to help you become a better human being. A better human being is someone who is self—sufficient, motivated, confident and never looking down at anyone "*ever*." However, make sure you return the same teaching to others who also require help.

100 It can also be considered an "Outer Dimension" where our understanding of physics is very different

101 Book II: Time is an Illusion

Whatever your personal belief is: spiritual, religious, or otherwise, our job is to attempt to make our world a better place to live in.

Love, as well as compassion, have become my greatest degree of inner tranquility and it has put my mind at ease. Love will help you remove whatever fear or insecurity you may have. It will give you the strength to cope with any obstacles you may encounter.

It is futile to harbour any hate or animosity towards those who betray or hurt us. Doing the opposite is far more constructive but it will drive them crazy. You are addressing the real problem, not complaining and moreover, you are healing your wounds.

You all want to feel good, consciously and unconsciously. Do you agree? You want to feel more complete, more satisfied plus more enlightened. Your time here on Earth, as I have mentioned, is a vacation. How you spend your vacation is all up to you. You can follow your original "*Blue Print*"[102] instinct with your thinking and reasoning in how you want your vacation to go. Nevertheless, because we have a wide range of choices, many of our decisions turn out wrong, and as a result, that makes you feel less complete and less satisfied. The problem is that most of you give up, instead of continuing to use your thoughts to connect yourself with the Universe. You must stay sharp enough to find its secret of making every choice a good one.

What I[103] wrote earlier is only for the few who, for hundreds of thousands of years, have found these secrets, this big Truth on what it takes to be happy, to quest for pleasure, wealth, love, and Power.

102 Refer to "Book II: Time is an Illusion", Chapter 2: My Awakening, subtitle "I Blue Print"
103 Not *"I"* as in my physical self, but *"I"* as in a Higher Source using my physical body.

It has been drawn on caves, written on stones, and on Ancient Scrolls. Most have been destroyed, some have been hidden, while others have still not been discovered.

You can find some of it in the Jewish text of the "*Haggadah*," the "*Torah*," the Christian "*Holy Bible*", the Islam "*Qu'rân*", the Buddhist text "*Mahauyutpatti*" the Hindu Holy book "*Vedas*" and the "*Ramayana*", the Sikh "*Guru Granth Sahib*",[104] or "*Adi Granth*", which are a holy scripture.[105] Some are written just now, or will be written tomorrow or in the near future. In each finding, you will find partial or incomplete logical knowledge. An example is the "*Kabbalah*". All the puzzles will slowly link as one.

This Secret Truth is the key that shall help you understand who you are, what life is, and learn the deep mystery that connects you all. What most do not know is that you, with the Universe, has never stopped growing as well as expanding, not even for a moment. I am here, and I have always been here, yet never as the same physical person and only with partial memories.

It is important to understand that this is who you really are. People like me, who have these special gifts, can see what others do not see or understand. Some will be phony pretenders. There will be a bunch of you that will doubt or even fear us, but deep down you know what I am saying is true. You are loaded with Spiritual Power, but it is up to you to unlock your access to it.

---

104 Punjabi: gurū granth sāhib

105 Bardo Thodol, Tibetan "Book of the Dead", The Book of Mormon — Latter Day Saints (Mormons), The Avesta — Zoroastrianism, The Qur'an and the Hadith — Islam, The authenticated writings of Bahaullah — Baha'I, The Bhagavad Gita — Hinduism, The Mahavira's oral teachings as recorded in 12 Angas and Up—angas — Jainism, The Three Baskets (Tipitaka) — Theravada Buddhism, The Vajrayana Tantra — Vajrayana Buddhism, The Tao—te Ching — Taoism, The Kojiki or Records of Ancient Events, and the Nihongi — Shintoism, The Torah, Talmud and Tanakh — Jews, Old Testament & New Testament — Christians.

Why is it that when we die, regardless of how, people remember us as Teachers, "*wise*" in "*knowledge*," but not before?

You decide how you want to see life and as a result how you want to live. To understand the Universe you must first understand yourself. Changing how you see your life, along with the world, is your first step.

My source of my wisdom is not my own, but a collection of other thoughts that float around me in visions and dreams. I believe something Higher than I shows me what to write, including my future self, because time is one time line. For years, I have been ignoring the gifts I have, for I was afraid. I can only use these gifts or receive them in time of need.

You may live, breathe, walk and talk, but most of the time, you do not use more than a fraction of your Spiritual Power. That is because you do not believe. You lost hope and faith. Look, for example, how people around you no longer even vote in your City or Country![106] Faith does not always come easily, but you wish that you could surrender yourself to it, am I right?

You are people who act as if you did not give up, yet you do. You are asked whether you know something or someone and you say you do not, when in reality, you do. You worry endlessly about how terribly limited your world is. The problem is you create it to be what you want it to be.

When you are asking, it is like praying. It comes in many forms. Asking is like a prayer that may come in many forms. Today your thoughts are your prayers as results so are the questions you ask yourself. You are expanding a union with the mysteries of your own heart. You may feel a bit lost, but when you ask for guidance, you

106 Being involved in their communities or any election votes.

receive it. You will probably find out in the process that you are not as bad off as you thought you were. You are closer to the goal now. You might even be the person who has started a certain project. However, someone else may take it over and lead things to a different direction than the one you would have chosen. This will not necessarily be a bad thing if it is successful. Learn to keep an open mind.

Wisdom and joy only come from learning how to see a wider, much more wondrous world, and power comes only from your thoughts in what you "*ASK, SEE, SEEK, BELIEVE,*" and then "*FEEL*" that you "*RECEIVED.*" Changing your vision in how you look at the world is the first step. You are require as well as must see that you are responsible in your creation.

Everything in your life happens for a reason. Every person, place, as well as event in your life is perfectly designed by your subconscious to teach you something you require to learn in order to be free.

The moment you opened this book and understand what has been written through my hands,[107] is the moment when you are ready to truly see the Truth to the secret that's been in front of you for hundreds of thousands of years. Not everyone will understand or accept this old Ancient knowledge. There are groups out there who want to keep you ignorant and so, as a result, deceive you with half—truths. So be careful, do your own research, and furthermore do not believe everything you read.[108]

The two Oldest Ancient Groups have always been the "*Ones*" and the "*Shadows*".[109] One group has always controlled the World's events

107 A Higher—Source.

108 Refer to Jake Hollow's "How to Deal with Emotions and the Life of a Motivational Speaker" Part I: Life—Coaches on Internal Damage, Chapter 2: Challenge, subtitle "I Directing My Message"

109 I first mentioned them in Jake Hollow's "How to Deal with Emotions and the Life of a Motivational Speaker" Part I: Life—Coaches on Internal Damage, Chapter 2: Challenge,

like the governments and the economy; the other, the world's wisdom and knowledge. Your choice is to be a part of the world or be in the world but not of it. You can only find the real you inside you, not in words, books, philosophies, or even religions. You have to solve it by being sharp and noticing all the hidden clues. Therefore, I am asking you to "*dissect*" these "*secret codes*" that will not only help you, but also help others. You must be patient and calm to receive what you ask for. It cannot be found by seeking, but only seekers will find it.

You tend to fight against the Truth of this natural Law of the Universe, so you suffer more and more because your thoughts only believe in the unbelievable and negativity of life. There are those who get all, power, success, fame, or riches they thought they wanted, but as a result instead of being happy, they soon destroy themselves.

Before you send your frequency to ask the Universe to understand your message, you must be at peace with yourself first. Every thought, fear, anger, or doubt that the Universe receives from you will fill your life, instead of the opposite.[110] This is not negotiable; it is the Universal Law of Creation and it behaves just like energy and gravity. In truth, you are all connected with the Universal Consciousness, but most of you cannot see it. Because of this, you create what you do not want. You are going against the Truth, against the natural flow of reality. This is your choice.

You are each responsible for how you live your life in this physical illusion. Each of you has the power to change it, if you truly believe without any doubt whatsoever. You create your own blessings or curses.

You are here on vacation for two purposes; one is to learn, the other is to live. You must become enlightened. Always have loving thoughts.

---

under subtitle "I Directing My Message"
110 Meaning your worth fears will become

Empty your mind of negative assumptions, attitudes, limitation and definitions. A mind that is open, free of fear, and free from unwanted thoughts is clear and powerful enough to deal with anything.

All physical existence is an illusion. The physical laws include energy, space, time, gravity, as well as evolution. There are other laws. The Secrets of the Universe, Multiverses or Outer Dimensions are only secrets if your thoughts are filled with negative energy.

Your thoughts require balance; you must honour a unique balance with yourself. The Universal Laws of Creation would seem to treat you all equally, but actually, any written law is changeable depending on your state of mind and Spirit.

How you feel will direct how the Universe translates your message. For example, if you are uptight while you are sending it, your frequency, will feed off you being uptight, then the signal can become scrambled, confusing to the Universe.

The Universe is unbiased. My point is that details are very important when you ask, but the detail in when you will receive it is not your worry. The moment you worry or doubt, you are sending it back.[111] It must come to you when you least expect it to arrive.

You must fully understand that the understanding the Universe picks up is in another language. It can misinterpret your "*wants*" to create the opposite. The problem is you may not want to know the Truth if your mind and heart are not working together. You may want to believe that you are asking the Universe what you want, but deep down you feel the opposite. You look for excuses and you repress your heart's requests. Work on getting yourself in tune with both your thoughts and feelings working as one.

111 As if you refused your package directly from your mail person

Now, let me ask you once again;

Do you have a problem making ten thousand dollars in a year (365 days) without even thinking or sweating?

If you answered '*yes*', then the same belief in one million dollars or more is the same concept.[112] Once you fully comprehend this belief, you can do and receive whatever you desire. I, for one, would like to see everyone being fully successful.

Faith is an antidote to fear.

If you lose your faith, the foundation of your creative endeavour will crumble.

Patience and faith go hand in hand.

Be certain when you submit your request to the Universe that your motive only serves and blesses all life and for the highest good, and that you are willing to go out and do your work to do your part to precipitate your own supply.

112 Chapter 3: Positive Thought

Chapter 8

The Vision Board

"Use a Vision Board to plan your way" — **Gino DiCaprio**

Most of you will find that the hardest and most important part is to know, without a doubt, that it has already happened. Not just faith that it will happen but knowing, in the core of your being, that it has happened.

You can visualize all you want but without the conviction that it already **IS**, than it **IS NOT**.

The best way to do this is to be grateful everyday, all day, for everything that you have.[113] Say how grateful you are that you have this thing and really feel that gratefulness and you will have it.

Gratefulness is especially important when you have doubts or are just feeling low or down for no reason at all. You can't be depressed and truly be grateful at the same time, it's not emotionally possible.

It starts small; you must have the eyes to see it!

113 Including the thing you desire to attract

I have manifested some things within a couple hours, some within a couple months, and others in a few years. Keep in mind that you shouldn't have any "*limiting beliefs*". A lot of this is found in the subconscious. Another is that you have to live in the **NOW**. By that I mean... don't think about it as being in the future and make sure your life on the outside is parallel with what you want... as in leave room in your closet with coat hangers for your new clothes.[114] Also, have fun and be happy now, don't think about what will happen later. **EXPECT IT**!

Why do you get what you want sometimes, and at other times, what you want eludes you?

Why are some born rich, while others poor?

Why do some have great talent while others are limited in ability?

The truth is it is the same Universe however there are different realities. The differences are your thoughts on "*what you expect to have*", "*what you want*, or "*that you expect disaster at every turn*". Listen to your own thoughts. I mean listen to them clearly. Listen to your emotion. Now ask yourself,

Am I a positive thinker or not?

Do I expect the best or worry about the worst?

Seriously, look inside yourself.

Teach your children by having them use their imagination. Put up a board and have them place pictures of all the things they want, as well as then picture how they want their life to be.[115]

114 Metaphor

115 Refer to Jake Hollow's "How to Deal with Emotions and the Life of a Motivational Speaker" Part II: Defining Emotions Chapter 5: Words Can Lie The Body Cannot

Put this board in your kitchen where you can see it and look at it every day. See, Ask, Believe and feel it as if you have already Received it "**NOW**!" As you receive, and feel gratitude for having something, you can remove the old pictures and add new ones. I am having my children do this yet it is up to them to follow this game every day and make it fun.

Once you place your vision board up where you can see it, you do not have to look at it every moment you walk by it for your brain to continually pick it up and register it to your memory. An affirmation is not required to drive the idea deep into your subconscious mind.

If you believe that it is only your mind that is in control of your memories, you have forgotten that even your heart has memories. In other words, you must not only visualize with your mind through thoughts, what you created on your vision board, by thinking of it on a conscious level in the moment. You must also *FEEEEEL* it, *TAAASSSSSTTTTTE* it, *TOUUUUUUUCCCH* it, *SEEEEE* it as well as *BEEEELIIIIIEVVVVE* it deep in your heart. Sense that it is coming, as a result, is already here **NOW**.

Brain + Heart = Faster results.

Your subconscious mind, your eyes, your heart, as well as your whole being will absorb what it thinks, sees, feels, and senses even when you may believe you didn't look or even glance at your personal vision board you've put up.

Keep it in mind that the Universe will bring you what you demand when you least expect it to be or even better than what you would of expected once you've completely forgotten all about what you ordered. The Universe does not forget. In addition, it takes care of the details of "*when, where*" and "*how*". So stop your worries, and give it up to the Universal Law of Creation.

To achieve all that you want, you must consistently write your "*wills*" down in fine detail. Even if you have no inclination of a clue in how to start whatever it is you desire to build, do not get caught up in the details of "*how*".

Let the Universe deal with the details because if the Universe can re—arrange the entire Cosmos, then it can surely shuffle a few things around to make you happy by putting you at the right place at the right moment so that your wish can come true. Only if and when you fully trust it and pay attention when it puts opportunities in front of your face for you to take advantage of, will you actually see it. Do you follow?

Just be one hundred percent clear about what it is you want. Don't confuse the Universal Consciousness with what you do not want. Just let the Universe decide "*when*" with the details of "*how*. Let it do its job.

The Universe is all about expansion in growth. It loves you more than you could ever imagine. It wants you to be happy; it wants to give you what you want. In the end, it wants to give you what is best for you, and the Universe is never ... never wrong.

Make sure your heart is deeply involved with what you want. This should not be just your thoughts, however but all of you. All that you desire, all that you wish shall, and will, come true only once you fully accept the idea that your whole being has to be truly, fully, as well as deeply involved along side of the Universe as one, beyond any shadow of a doubt. By this, all that you ask for will no longer be an illusion.

Do not make a move to figure out how your dreams shall come to be, do not plan how you shall reach or achieve your dreams, just leave it to the Universal Consciousness to figure it out; how it will happen and be delivered to you. Let the Universe devise the most unexpected way to put it in front of you so that you can notice your opportunity.

All "*you*" are required to do is be aware when it is in front of you so that you can take advantage of it. Then you can plan your success in a fashionable order. Meditate hard on what you just read.

Remember the Universe will help and put in place what you ask for, however it will not hold your hand. The Universe wants you to do your part and that which is to "*work*" for what you want. Not work hard but to work smart and to stay focused.

Nevertheless, there will be times that the Universe will take its time; it may take longer to provide it than you might expect.

This may get you to start questioning if this Ancient belief is real and really working. This can result in doubt as well as your selfish personal needs. Whatever you do, do not do this! This will destroy your real focus, and by doing this… at that moment, you just "*cancelled*" the order you demanded.

Are you following me or just pretending to be?

By having doubts, you have now insulted as well as offended the Universal Laws of Creation. Remember that in the physical reality you live by what is called "*time space*". It is a continuum in which events occur while the Universe does not, for time is "*one*" and it foresaw in advance that you did not truly believe in it. It felt that your belief was not true, it was not selfless, but selfish in nature. For that you "*slapped*" away what you wanted in a tidal wave.

Again stay focussed. Let the Universe deal with "*when, where*" and with the "*details*" for you. Whatever you may require, whatever you ask for, or for whomever you should meet for personal or business reasons, it will be there at the right moment, yet not when you expect it.

All becomes real only when you least expect it, because when it is unexpected, it automatically becomes "*not*" selfish. The theory is: Your subconscious never forgets all that you consciously visualized. Your subconscious automatically sent out frequencies to the Universal Consciousness through your thoughts and heart in a selfish/selfless way, that way you are not only helping yourself, but also you're helping others.

A miracle itself is inexplicable. When you truly believe, it all just falls into place. Do you follow? When you are connected along side with the Universe, you become energized. In addition your vibrational frequency becomes pure, and by this, all that you want shall flow towards you in abundance. You shall be on a High Energy Frequency. As a result, things will happen for you much more easily and fall into place more than ever before.

You become the creator of your life; you are surrounding yourself with the Universal Force, since that is what flows towards you. All you are required to do is just be clear in what you want, and imagine that it is already at your disposal; in front of you in the flesh until it truly does manifest. Let it go so that the Universe can now make it real as in solid when you are not looking or paying it attention. It shall find the best way to give you what you want and desire. Do not be anxious[116] for it.

Your mind is the consciousness that directs your mental and physical behaviour. Your heart is the emotional center, such as love, hate, consideration, or compassion of the whole.

By all this, I hope you understand where I am going with this?

You bring towards you the energy of abundance by creating and then repeatedly visualizing exactly what you want to see happening in your

116 Worried about some uncertainty (negative feeling).

life. You can maximize the effectiveness of your prayers, affirmations, and meditations by summoning the power of your inner vision.

In your meditations, trance and prayers, visualize the desired outcome of your prayers. See what you must accomplish in every area of your life, including family, home, career, finances, health, education, relationships, and Spirituality.

Visualize the resolution of difficult situations. Be as specific as possible in your visualizations. The more centered, concentrated and creative you are, the better your result will be.

When you keep your thoughts anchored to the great Spiritual Being that you are, that image repels all that oppose the manifestation of your reality.

What image do you have of yourself?

If you list a lot of qualities that are less than positive, realize that you are attracting that 'less—than—positive' image to yourself, as every minute, hour and day of your life you are creating who you are. Whatever you visualize yourself to be, you will become.

Feedback from others is important, because you do not always realize how you come across to other people. It is beneficial to be able to see yourself through the eyes of another, yet you are not helping yourself if you look at yourself exclusively from the outside in.

It is essential that you live with the self—image not only of who you are right now, but also of who is your divine self. There is a part of you that recognizes the Spiritual Being that you are, and that you can become more of each day.

I. The One and Only

I HAVE GONE THROUGH A dramatic change in my life, but now I am working on living a neutral—positive[117] life. I am at peace with who I am. I am now seen as a Life—Coach, a Guru, a Spiritual Teacher, and the list goes on, and on.

I have changed my name quite a few times to dissociate myself from the old me. I was referred to as the High Adamant Counsellor and Advisor L—rd Master DiCaprio.[118]

I want to help you live out a neutral—positive life, being at peace with what you have. I want to relay this message to you. Whatever you do have, be grateful for it. When you feel you do not have enough money in the bank, be grateful for the money you do have.

When you feel you are stuck at a dead—end job, be grateful to have a job and work on improving your work environment. Learn to see the neutral and positive in all you believe to be negative, for you create the life you want. Learn to live in the life you have as well as learn how to create it and change it. You project the life you want unconsciously because of your hidden fears.

It is good to re—start your life by putting your old life and name to rest and picking up a new life and name. Change your name at least once to your new beginning, put your new history separate from the personal past you are leaving behind. [119]

If you have a group of people that uses neutral—positive thought waves, the more neutral or positive things will come. If you are around

117 Is also referred as Balance

118 Do not take this literary since it is an inside joke, where inmates' kept referring me too this title. I however made it clear I was not comfortable with it. See also Book III: Illuminatis The Ones and The Shadow.

119 Refer to Chapter 16: How Do You Start? Subtitle "I Where Are You Now?"

people who think negatively and their thoughts are over run by negative thoughts, the more negative vibes will come your way. The Universe takes order from your subconsciousness, so your subconscious belief is crucial.

I hope you followed this and took notes.

Chapter 9

The Universe Will Open for You

"Follow your bliss and the universe will open doors where there were only walls." — **Joseph Campbell**

The Creator of all existence created the Universe (Multiverses) so that it can support everything you do and meet all your requirements immediately, yet the question remains:

Are you having negative or neutral—positive[120] thoughts?

Never let your emotions get in the way of contacting the Universe by meditation or trancing. Witness your thoughts, allow your thoughts to come in, but again do not let your emotions interfere with your process.

If you base your life on emotions, they can get you off track. The purpose is to work from your heart, not your fears and worries. Those are useless emotions. Let your thoughts come in and let them go. Do

120 These are "Labels" that as humans we use. Same as "good" or "evil", "Spiritual Realm" or "Outer Dimension".

not get involved emotionally, but just watch and view without any emotion. Use your logic with your belief.

Let me use an extreme example to explain what I mean by emotional. Let's say that you are in a prison detention center for a crime you did not commit, but somehow you were involved in knowledge.[121] Meaning even if you weren't involved physically in the crime, you knew that those that you associate with were making money illegally which you were just looking the other way. You, however, were encouraging them to get clean and go fully with the law in other ventures, which was mistakenly taken as you were involved in their other business.

Now you are asking or praying;[122] "*I want to be home and free*". Your emotions of not wanting to be where you presently are, are involved, so what the Universe interprets is; "*I want to stay in jail and not go home*".

You are now saying;[123]

WHAT?

Your emotions are focused on your worst fear, which is not getting out sooner. You are making yourself believe you will be found guilty. By not being emotional, and dealing with your heart with logic, you should say and believe with your whole heart; "*I'm home in my house with my loved ones, and I'm acquitted on all charges*". With logic, you have no doubt of where you stand.

Ask by commanding the Universe and let it know what you want, not what you do not want. You may yell; "*I DO NOT WANT TO GO TO JAIL*" or "*I DO NOT WANT TO BE IN JAIL!*"

121 Using my own experience that I went through.
122 In a detention or prison.
123 WORDS are POWERFUL! Use your "words" carefully, do not take them for granted.

Yet in reality, you are unconsciously telling the Universal Consciousness your worst fear in; "*I WANT TO GO TO JAIL*" and "*I WANT TO BE IN JAIL!*"

Because of your fear, subconsciously you believe you shall be in jail, even if consciously you do not desire it or want to. Therefore, do not let your fear control you, in addition condition both your subconscious and unconscious minds to think like your conscious mind and become a Superconscious mind that thinks like; "*I AM FREE AT HOME WITH MY LOVED ONES*". You're your thoughts, you are visualizing being free and at home with your loved ones, but then out of nowhere your thought unexpectedly changes. The scene you are now viewing is the opposite to what you want.

By being anxious,[124] it shows you are worried and uncertain in which case it can result in a negative self—fulfilling prophecy.

Believe that your wish is already here in the **NOW** and not tomorrow. You have to act, speak, and think as though you received it **NOW**! The Universe is a mirror, and the Universal Law of Creation is mirroring back to you your dominant thoughts. The Past, Present and Future are "*ALL*" present as "*NOW!*"

Therefore, if you act and think as if you do not have it now, you attract the fact that it is not with you and that it will not be there with you. Make believe you already have it, until it becomes real.

Never worry about any of the details in how it will reach you for anyone that has "*made*" it in this world, they just believed and knew they were going to do it and did not worry about how.

124 Wanting changes right away. The Universe knows the right moment since there "may" be a lesson for you to learn about yourself.

How the Universe brings it to you is not your concern.[125] Just believe you have received it. It will not take time for the Universe to manifest what you want deep in your heart and mind. Expect what you want, and delete from both your heart and mind what you do not want, which is your subconscious fear.

The "*Law of Decree*", commands that what you project will happen no matter what, for your subconscious will see to it. So, if your conscious is stronger in negative thoughts, you will draw negativity towards you, and that is what you shall receive.

Meditation or trance is the same.

Do you let it take you over?

Do you let your emotion take over, and you become depressed and lose hope?

NOOooo! NO! ARE YOU A LOSER?

Let that negative scene in your mind play itself out, do not fight it, but embrace it. View it without any emotion; view it as an obstacle, which you have the solution to solve. Slowly, day by day you will eliminate all negatives and replace them with positives thoughts.

Do not look at negative as bad, but look at it as a positive that you can use and transform to your advantage. To one extent, one knows like the ancient wise man, and one becomes like him.

125 Joseph or Yosef (Standard Yosef Tiberian Yôsēp, Arabic: Yusuf; "May Yahweh add") was the eleventh of Jacob's twelve sons in the Holy Torah (Hebrew Bible) Christian Bible and the Qur'an. Joseph was sold into slavery by his jealous brothers, but "years" later rose to become the most powerful man in Egypt after Pharaoh. Patience is a virtue (Is this also not close to Jesus story?).

Roman Brave would say; "*If you behave like a g—d, you will become like a G—d.*"

Every morning make an effort to say; "*I AM SO HAPPY AND GRATEFUL NOW!*"

Make it a habit until this becomes **YOU**. Focus only on what you want, so that the Universe does not get confused with mixed messages. Do not ever bring doubts into your conscious, subconscious, and unconscious mind ever. I do mean ever, or you will have to re—start your command all over again. Combine them into one, so that you use your Superconscious to overcome it all.

Begin to feel wonderful as if your wish had arrived, feel the way you will feel once it arrived, and feel it NOW! Learn to turn your fantasies into reality, into a fact, without a shadow—of—a—doubt whatsoever in your whole being.

It takes no effort or time for the Universe to manifest what you want, no matter its size. However the moment you question it, is the moment you are showing that you doubt yourself, at the same time you are slapping away your request, which you should have received. So send this negative thought away, and replace it with, "*I KNOW I AM RECEIVING IT NOW,*" in addition, *FEEEEEL* it.

Expectation is a powerful attraction force, so expect the things you want, and not the things you do not want, by conditioning your mind to believe with total faith. Smile and be positive or even neutral about being happy and grateful **NOW**. The shortcut to anything you want in your life is to be and feel happy **NOW**! It is the fastest way to bring you anything you want into your life.

See what you want as an absolute fact. When you finally truly focus on what you want, what you surely do not want will fade away, and what you expect will expand.

People who set their mind on the negative dark side of life, who repeatedly relive their misfortunes and disappointments of the past, subconsciously pray for similar misfortunes and disappointments in their present and in their future.

Therefore, if you go back over your life, dwell and focus on the difficulty from your past, you are just bringing more circumstances that are difficult to you **NOW**. Let it go, let it all go, no matter what it is, or what it may be. Just let it go. Do you follow?

The secret is: do the things you love because this brings you total joy. If you have no clues on what can bring you joy, than ask yourself;

What is my joy?

Once you find it, commit yourself to it. The Universal Law of Creation will pour an avalanche of joyful things, people, circumstances, events, and opportunities into your life, all because you are radiating joy.

Follow your bliss and for you, the Universe will open doors where there used to be only walls and obstacles in your way. Then you can, will, and have the things people once said were impossible for you to do, have, or be. Do you follow where this is going?

I believe in you, my readers. I believe that you are great, that there is something magnificent about you.[126] Regardless of what has happened to you in your life, how old or young you may be.

126 Refer to "Book II: Time is an Illusion", Chapter 7: Equal Recognition

You will feel it the moment you begin to think properly, this something that is within you; this power within you that is greater than the world, will begin to emerge.

When you let this power in, it will take over your life, it will feed you, clothe you, guide you, protect you, direct you, and sustain your very existence. Now that is what I surely know.

The natural order of the Universal Laws has been written in a visible natural manner all around you. The Universe, in addition the force binds us all. There is an energy force that unites us all.

You are all physically connected; the molecules in your body are intertwined with the molecules in my body. There is a single force moving within all of you.

If you are someone who believes in the Holy Text then you believe that G—d created all that exist out of nothing. There was emptiness and nothing existed, so know that I am explaining that "you can create matter out of nothing. Matter is nothing but trapped energy, together with pure energy is the father of creation."

If you want something badly, then ask for it several times a day for a minimum of seven consecutive days.

Release all doubts and fears from within you. Do not try, you just **DO**! You shall get what you are asking for or something even better.

Make your request open—ended. If you ask for (…?),[127] but you received differently… this is because the Universe "knows" that (…?) is better. Do not think that the Universe did not answer you, for that

127 Fill in your own "desires".

will bring doubt in any future requests. In other words, let the Universe decide what the best answer is, and that is what you shall always get.

If you do visualize and question or doubt your will in—between any of those seven days, you must start all over again. You should also do this if you obtain your request before the seven days are finished. This often happens, yet you must still ask for the entire seven days. This is for those who believe with faith and confidence.

The Supreme Being is not some omnipotent authority looking down from above, and threatening to throw you into a pit of fire if you disobey. This Higher Power is the energy that flows through the synapses of your nervous system as well as the chambers of your heart! This Universal Consciousness is everywhere and is present in all things!

You attract towards you whatever you give your invisible vibrating energy and attention to, whether you do it consciously or not. Do you follow my meaning on this?

What you focus on becomes your reality.

Through your thoughts, power and will, you attract into your life everything you desire. Focus on what I am writing, for when you think of the same thing over and over and over again, good or bad, that is what you are calling out for. Do you follow?

Therefore, if you let negative thoughts overtake your life, you are sabotaging all your good work you have been asking for.

The most Powerful Ancient method has been around since time started as an echo that repeats itself. "*Repeating*" brings affirmation, which declares that you stand by your truth that this is what you truly deserve.

By repeating strongly all your inner emotions, you "*will*" attract all that you want. Otherwise, once you train how your subconscious mind should think automatically by your conscious view without doubt whatsoever, you "*will*" have full control as if you had a Genie at hand. You shall no longer think about what you desire in a conscious level, because it will be an automatic reflex. You will subconsciously become a KnoWing.[128]

I. Building from Scratch

When all is going wrong in your life, it is because of two reasons:

One: you subconsciously sabotage yourself.

Or

Two: someone sinister is sabotaging you.

At this moment do not blame others, but take full responsibility for your own predicaments and yell aloud from the top of your lungs; "*THAT IS ENOUGH, I GET IT, I GOT THE MESSAGE, IT IS TOO DEEP, AND I DO NOT HAVE TO PUT UP WITH THIS ANYMORE!*"

You will prevent more pain from coming your way. At the same time you will heal the old problem by putting a positive solution to it, which is neutral. You must first care for yourself completely, even while those who do not understand this, some may think that you are being self—centered by doing just what we mentioned for you to do.

128 Refer to "Book II: Time is an Illusion", Chapter 2: My Awakening, subtitle " II Our Spiritual Plain of Existence"

Follow my instructions and test this for one to two weeks. State everything that you wish to do. I will guarantee that by the end of the first or second week, you will not only be doing your wills for yourself, but you will be doing more for others as well.

Why?

"*Because of passion*", as Roman Brave would say. We all must appreciate who we are and this can begin with a self—gift of acknowledgment. The move to self takes very little effort but it brings a wealth of love from you that begins to emanate in all directions.

Yes, it might seem selfish, but not in this format, for there is only fear that causes a person to become introverted[129] and closed off to others.

In your mind, you must build and visualize hard and deep, a place you are building from scratch of a size that feels comfortable and right for you. Where you can go to receive counselling, healing, and any other help with any type of difficulties you may have. This way you can create and help yourself with solving whatever obstacle is giving you problems, with a positive outcome.

In your mind, you must create that reality for yourself and for us. The more details you give, the stronger its existence will be for you, that is the secret. Complete this before you fall asleep that way you will create a mind—place to sleep.

Once all details like windows, flowers, bright colours and so on are all done, start to feel them. Surround yourself to really being there. Truly sense and feel it deep in your being. You are there without any

129 One whose thoughts and interests are directed inward.

doubts. Feel yourself starting to become a whole, with a new feeling of stability, power, and control in your life.

In your mind, go as far as sitting down or lying down on a comfortable couch to relax along with talking to a Spiritual Master Guru in your mind. Ask for help but only one physical problem at a time on each session. Surrender yourself totally. Furthermore, identify your problem; while you are doing this, it is also alright to finally fall asleep in the physical reality.

You may also bring a loved one mentally into your place of healing; of course, you must create the room that your loved one would feel comfortable with. Then, place them there, and ask your Spiritual Master Guru to help you.

There is no limit to what you can do using this scenario. The only block you may encounter is if the other person physically does not want that help. You must respect their free choice.

If you sense that outside forces are manipulating your loved one psychologically then you must find those sources and eliminate them. This technique can heal both of you; therefore, you can get others involved so that the energy will be stronger, in helping you.

When returning back to the physical realm, see that you enjoy life. Every moment you find a chance without caring if anyone is around or not; I want you to shout aloud;

"I LOVE MY LIFE AND LIFE LOVES ME, LIFE, AS WELL AS ALL GOOD THINGS LIKE FINANCIAL WEALTH, MY HEALTH AS WELL AS HAPPINESS WITH LOVE IS DRAWN TO ME LIKE A MAGNET!"

Truly and really, believe with love when you scream this out loud. Do not feel ashamed or embarrassed by this, for if you do, you are going against the Universal Law of Creation.

Keeping yourself focused on what you want is extremely important. It must be "*pure*," it must be "*real*." Build a strong relationship with what you desire, in what you want, in what you demand, do not treat it like your old dysfunctional relationship you used to have before you started reading this book.

Do not, and I mean "**DO NOT**" yell your words I have asked you to with an "*empty hollow*" heart. Do you understand?

Be brave, be a warrior as well as be courageous for "*you are greatness among greatness*" and never forget that.

What you demand stays with you when you "*respect, cherish*" and "*love*" it. The more you "*feel*" love, not "*think*" love, but truly sincerely "*feel*" love way deep within your being, the more "*powerful*" your magnet will become. In fact, you attract towards you more and better things to you.

Chapter 10

Learn To Stretch Your Mind

"All that we are is the result of what we have thought. If a man speaks or acts with an evil thought, pain follows him. If a man speaks or acts with a pure thought, happiness follows him, like a shadow that never leaves him." — **Buddha**

What I write is all a puzzle that only a few will figure out; a few of you will be able to partly put it together. However, most will profess to believe they can interpret what was written through my hands by flashing their credentials or perhaps a degree of education in anthropology, philosophy, religiology,[130] or human behaviour yet all of them shall not even be close. Only those who are truly connected outside modern society and in tune with their Spiritual—Self from the untold time and space, will be close to figuring it out.[131]

130 Knowledge on a wide range of Meyhaphisics, Ethnology, Archaeology, Sociology, Politology, and others practical work of specialists.

131 Refer to "Book III: Illuminatis The Ones and The Shadows"

I've have studied all kinds of philosophies, such as Socrates, and religious text such as the Hebrew Torah, the different Christian versions of the Bible, the Islamic Qu'rân etcetera. It is surprising how all or most philosophers and religions are similar in their approaches.

I want to make it clear that I'm not here to bring a new age belief, nor advocate any religion in any form, but to bring to your notice a belief that's been around longer than humankind has been writing; something that has been long forgotten by modern man. I refer to a time when, if it was written, it would not be worth remembering.[132]

One must learn to be aware of the power of their emotions, how not to be overwhelmed by extremes that are sometimes felt. A lot of people have labelled me as a Life—Coach and Spiritual Teacher, even thou I personally don't accept these titles I can still be of assistance by showing you the way, however you have to find your own way to your destination. Therefore, the less emotional baggage you take with you, the easier it will be. Questions are acceptable; however, you must pay very close attention to your "*questions*" seeing that the "*answers*" are right in front of you "*in*" your own questions. [133]

Be cautious of those who tell you they can help you and piggy you on their back,[134] for I don't believe in laziness. I believe that you practice until you become great at it, not only good at it, for anyone can be good at it, but being great is perfection at its best.

Like those who keep their bodies in perfect shape, you should do the same with your mind, by learning to stretch both your body and mind in ways you had not, ever imagined possible.[135]

---

132 I shall be mentioning this quite a few time in the following chronicles. Book II: Time is an Illusion and Book III: Illuminatis The Ones and The Shadows.

133 Especially in "Spiritual" questions.

134 They make you feel as if you "must" rely on them word for word.

135 Before reading this book.

By learning to meditate or trance, you will see in time that due to the training you will perform well without spending much time in your outside work or school. Since your mind will be so clear and focused, you will be able to study for only a small while, confident that you can recall the knowledge at will.

The "*Universal Law of Manifestation*" attracts what you mirror deep down in your subconscious mind.

I. Our Possible Future

PROPHECIES HAVE GUIDED PEOPLE THROUGHOUT history in some vibrational way to make a profound connection or revelation between the so called past and what is yet to come. As a Visionary, I have the ability to go into an altered state of consciousness and remember ancient times before history was even written, a time we believed that "*if it was written then it was not worth remembering*".

What I foresaw in our near future is that time will be very difficult for many of you. You will have to adapt to a new consciousness of change, forced upon you in how you live. This will be the time when you will have no choice but to wake up.

You will clear away the old patterns that have held you imprisoned in this dark time. It will take little by little, just like a drop of water, for these hidden secrets to be revealed on your quest to understand these prophetic messages. [136]

Most of the knowledge remains in my memory of time. Most were given by oral facts, which have been handed down through

136 Refer to "Book III: Illuminatis The Ones and The Shadows"

generations. I shiver with anticipation for what I know to come; I am waiting for that moment when there will be no cycle of time.

If you all envision your possible future, you can create the outcome. Once you see it as well as truly believe it, the power you have at your fingertips will be virtually unlimited. So, I advise you to dream and make your thoughts into a reality.

We have kept these secrets from the mass for hundreds of thousands of years, but now we are giving you, the masses, a chance to change even the direst predictions on the thread of time. With your focus, and if you are all awakened, it is possible. I know that as a Visionary, Creator, you can bring out what you want, however it is up to each of you to make it happen.

I have come to understand that this is the reason I am here, why I am required here. I have been reincarnated[137] for these outcomes. I have always been here; this is why I am alive physically and the reason things happen as they do.

I urge you to look to the not too distant future where you will be fully restored amongst a significant critical mass of beings. I can confirm that you are here to awaken your senses of Spirituality in preparation for the coming changes here on Earth.

You will restructure the damaged energies to heal, so that you can become more whole and less fragmented. You must be aligned with the frequency of the Universe, for it is love. As human beings, you can only carry a limited memory span of one life at a time,[138] while the rest shows in dreams and visions.[139]

---

137 Embodied in a new mortal form, since I have "always been".

138 If you are over thirty years old, can you remember "every" single day you had at ten years old? Then how can you remember all your previous physical life, if you can't remember this one.

139 Refer to "Book II: Time is an Illusion", and "Book III: Illuminatis The Ones and The Shadows"

If I was only meditating, would I be fulfilling my mission?

My decision was made. I urged myself to train for what is to come. When things become tough, I will take myself up. Those with the gifts will find me and help direct me subconsciously.

I am required to complete this mission[140] in the present to secure the future. If I was to ask you to see what you call the future, you would see what you might never have imagined, not even in your wildest dreams. How things may work out in a certain manner, I have no idea, only a thought that by chance it may.

I invite you to walk with me on this path over the edge of Time, where there is no knowing what may happen, where, or when. You will have to be clear in what you want to do now, in the present, as it is important. Parting the strands of Time and then weaving them into a whole vision for the future is never easy, even for us. Wisdom may be found without struggle or effort. All is an illusion in perception.

I want to let you, my readers, know from the start that I no longer have time for pleasantries and small talk. I have a message for people genuinely seeking answers. I will tell you all now that I have quit apologizing for what I believe in. If that is a ground rule you can live with, I have all the time you crave.

Just as you lift weights in the gym to build up your physical muscles, you must repeatedly bring your awareness back to your breath to develop your mental muscles.

140 Refer to "Book III: Illuminatis The Ones and The Shadows"

II. Ahead of Their Time

THERE ARE RARE AND EXTRAORDINARY unique beings like Y'shua[141] as well as others, and not all of them known. Even worse, they have been erased from history. They were rare and precious beings. Their message became largely misunderstood also greatly distorted from the Truth and real message.[142]

Back when they were alive, the world was not ready for them. They were looked on as g—ds and more advanced beings, but they were misunderstood. Their teachings, although both simple as well as powerful, became distorted and misinterpreted. In some cases, even as they were being recorded, in writing, by their followers and disciples. Over the centuries, many things were added that had absolutely nothing to do with their original teachings. [143]

I am not here to advocate any religion or religious belief. How Spiritual I am has nothing to do with what I believe in, however it has everything to do with my state of consciousness. This, in turn, determines how I act in the world, as well as interact with others.[144]

You do not become good by acting good, but by finding the goodness that is already within you, by allowing that goodness to emerge.

141 Hebrew for Joshua, which Christian calls Jesus. The Oldest Greek Text Did not have IESOUS for the MessiYah's name but simply IU, You can view this at: (www.codexsinaiticus.org/en/) Mathews Chapter 1:1 Reads as follows: is the original Transliteration not IESOUS which latter was added just like "L—rd, and G—d" was a substitution for YHWH and Elohiym. Since the Greek alphabet LACKED the necessary letters to transliterate the name properly there can be not proper transliteration from Hebrew to Greek of the Messiyah's name. Thus transliteration using IESOUS is not a Valid Transliteration which makes the name Yesus and/or Jesus also in valid. When one pronounces the name JESUS, it is properly pronounced in the Late Latin as HEY ZEUS. Latins are sea people who are related to the Greek/Crete family of people. Zeus is their god and the King of the gods of the Greek Mythology.

142 Refer to "Book II: Time is an Illusion", and "Book III: Illuminatis The Ones and The Shadows"

143 Refer to "Book II: Time is an Illusion", Chapter 8: Translation, subtitle "I Reflect On This"

144 Refer to Chapter 10: Learn To Stretch Your Mind, and Book II: Time is an Illusion, Chapter 1: Corporeal.

III. In Your Command

THE WORLD WE LIVE IN is a place of physical matter that is not real; it is an illusion that I call "*un—real*". This illusion is as if you are in a dream—state, and must only become awakened with awareness. This may happen once a person experiences a near death experience. At this point, you may begin your next reincarnation in the next life that you may or may not choose.[145]

Those of you who are truly awakened will become one with the Universe and its outgoing purpose. Your thoughts will inspire the system, and it will flow into what you do, which will guide, and empower you, in fulfilling your destiny.

There are certain ways that you can intertwine and align your life with the Creative Power of the Universe. Once you have awakened and are aware of the following fact, you must have total acceptance, enjoyment and enthusiasm; this will provide a positive vibrational frequency of consciousness to the Universe.

Some of you become awakening aware only through persistent negative thoughts you have had in your life.

You desire to feel the importance of True Inner acceptance no matter what you do. This means taking full responsibility for your life. Through enjoyment, you will link your desires into Universal Creative Power itself.

You want to sense and feel the joy of being, your ability to enjoy what you do; and without waiting for it, you will send a pure frequency to the Universe.

---

145 Refer to "Book II: Time is an Illusion", Chapter 2: My Awakening, subtitles "I Blue Print" and Chapter 3: Seven (7) Spiritual Levels.

Instead of waiting for some change, positive change is more likely to come into your life when you enjoy what you are doing. The Universe must feel that your joy does not come from what you do, but that it should "*flow*" into what you do "*deep within you*" as a sense of aliveness. That aliveness must be one with who you are.

You demand to be absolutely one hundred percent without any doubt whatsoever, being alert, alive, and present.

If you want the Universe's total attention, you will have to work towards your vision as a goal with enthusiasm so that the Universe can fully understand your vibrational frequency and enjoy the journey. Learn to accept, but do not worry or become stressed out for it will confuse the Creative Power of the Universe. Enthusiasm is one with life; you use it to enter into full alignment with the outgoing Creative Principle of the Universe.

For the Universe to follow your command and wish, you must have goals for what you are doing in the NOW. These goals must be your main focus or you will fall out of alignment with the Universe.

Feel yourself being open and, through you your energy flows all life for the benefit of all. You may only manifest what you already have, however to get what you want is through hard work. What you ask for; should not only enrich or deepen only you, but countless others.

The thought of abundance coming only to those who already have it may sound unfair, except it is not. When the opportunity is in front of you, you must take it.

It is a Universal Law. It will just manifest as your reality. Remember that all things that are labelled as good or bad are just an illusion. Once there is inspiration, and enthusiasm, there is a Creative Empowerment in your Alignment which Intertwines with the Universe. Through the power of NOW, your cycle of rebirth happens and you become internally aligned with space.

If in any way you find that '*Part I: Secrets and Laws of the Universe*' is incomprehensible or meaningless, then the awareness of being awaken has not yet happened to you, and you should not be looking forward to the next chronicle.[146] If you somehow recognize the Truth then continue to read on, it means the process of being awaken has begun. Awareness is conscious connection with the Universal Intelligence.

The Higher Power is able to do, exceed, and surpass all that you ask or think, according to the Power that works in you. You can do all things, the Universe Strengthens you, the Power is not of you but from this Higher Source. "*I think I can*" will not gain its solution, however to "*I declare I know I can*" will.

Buddha, G—d, Hashem, Yahweh, the Singularity, the Unicity Point, the list goes on and on. Call it whatever you like, the result is the same. "*If you like it, I love it*", Ernst (Miami) Appolon would say.

146 Refer to "Book II: Time is an Illusion and Book III: Illuminatis The Ones and The Shadows"

Chapter 11

Passion Should Be Your Goal

"Live with passion! ... Setting goals is the first step... Stay committed to your decisions, but... Success comes from taking the initiative..."
— **Tony Robbins**

The Universe has an "*order*" which follows many different laws, and the "*Universal Law of Creation*" is one law that deals with the OUTS as well as the INS of the Universe. Do you follow where I am going with this?

There are many Universal Laws; however, you have to stay focused in your vibrational frequencies, by raising them by thinking of things you can do to shift your subconscious in order to attract the things you want.

Everything comes down to energy. By reading over my own words,[147] I realized that I may have understood my soul connection

147 Not truly my words, but from a Higher Source.

from the very beginning, and that I have allowed my mind to interfere with that connection from quite a negative place.

I have seen the error of my ways and am working to do what I can to turn it around. You may wonder for yourself if it's possible (too late) and feel a bit of shame from seeing your own words in mine.[148] Since you did not believe your own actions until now, it is never too early nor too late. It is when you are ready and not a moment before.

There are those of you who have asked me;

Q: Why do you always say:
"The answer is all around you."
"The answer is there for you to see."
Yet, I don't see it.
A: It is called the "*KnoWing*". You lose it when you are thinking. It's, for example, as if you are somewhere yet somehow for only a "*split*" second something tells you to leave, but you don't and then a few minutes later a huge disaster comes into "*your*" life.

Q: Is every answer always there for us, is that what you are saying?
A: Yes

Q: We have our own answers; you, or anyone else, cannot answer things for others?
A: Correct.

I would like to think of myself as confident, humble, outgoing, yet not pushy or self—promoting. I am sure that there are a few people out there who believe the opposite about the concept of myself, following their own view of justification. I, on the other hand, know that there is no wrong nor right in both beliefs or views.

148 "Mine" is a metaphor, since it was written by a Higher Source through my hands.

I have come to be at peace with myself. I have become gentler, kinder. I also believe and have hope now. This is a serenity about myself I never would have believed possible to achieve years ago. I used to be a "*me*" person first.

I would like you, my readers, to look deep into yourselves and ask;

How and what can I do to feel good, even if things around me are in crazy negative chaos?

My answer to you is that you do have a choice in how you deal with your thoughts. Now you are asking;

Thoughts! What do thoughts have to do with this?

To create, you must think thoughts as in Emanating,[149] am I correct?

My solution is: *I can help you find certain ways to shut down negative thoughts from your mind.*

How and why?

MOST OF YOU FOCUS ON the negative of your past, which affects you in the "*now*" moment. Everything around you is energy with different vibrations, so because of this you're drawn to people who are like you. If you don't like being with these people, then it should be your goal to commit yourself to find and associate with those who are really at your level of neutral—positive thoughts. Otherwise, when you are a complainer, you will be surrounded by complainers. Do you follow so far?

We all demand to find those who have the same frequency as us.

149 Chapter 1: Logic and Belief.

Let us use the animal kingdom as an illustration in the "*Universal Law of Creation*" at work. A flock of ducks flies North to South in the winter and South to North in the spring. Yet, you will not see the wild geese mixing with the ducks for they work on different frequencies.[150] Each species in the animal kingdom has a different frequency, the Universe works in a perfect order. This is the "*Law of Order*". Do you comprehend this? I have been told to be careful with this example; one can argue that, according to my comparison, black and white races are different. That is not what I am saying, yet I do welcome constructive criticism on the topic; people do not have to agree or create what they feel is justified. I feel comfortable with this paragraph.

The "*Law of Perpetuation*"[151] states that energy of thoughts can turn into material energy. You must send this energy of thoughts to the Universe, so that your dominating thoughts predominate.

This law goes from a higher frequency to a lower frequency to become real and manifest itself.

The "*Law of Perpetual Transmutation*", brings energy of thoughts into material energy; it is related to transmuting energy for every thought. Your dominant thoughts are beginning to send that message to the Universe.

In a very short time, that message goes out to your subconscious mind and takes shape in material form, at

Spiritual level in a
Physical body through a
Creative process.

150 Even if they are headed to the same destination.
151 Last indefinitely.

We are Spiritual Beings with entities (bodies) having human experiences.

You have to build a purposeful goal by being specific and having a deadline. The "*Law of Incubation*" will give you time to manifest itself when you least expect it. Spiritual seeds are in your subconscious mind. You have to nurture your seeds in your subconscious mind by nurturing them with affirmation every day.

The "*Law of Gestation*"[152] is when the Universe brings people, events, and circumstance together.[153] Your goal is ready, your goal is growing, it will manifest in the physical realm, when the Universe is ready. Your job is to keep moving whatever you are guided to do; your job is to keep moving.

The "*Law of Justification*"[154] is when things "*should*" happen, but these do not happen when you want. Let the Universe worry about the details; it will deal with everything and everyone in the right place and at the right time. It will manifest on the day that it should and not earlier or later, regardless of your will. Therefore, stay focussed with a neutral—positive high vibration. Do not doubt it, with a lower negative vibration, for it is all in a perfect order.

The "*Law of Relativity*" is learning to share your neutral—positive waves about others with them and never with sadness. So, if a friend of yours buys a beautiful home,[155] show them how happy you are, with and for them. Do not compare what you have to their belongings, but share with them their success. Be creative, never jealous when being competitive,[156] and truly look at your situation — it could be worse.

152 Conception and development especially in the mind.
153 Pay close attention to your surroundings.
154 The process or result of justifying lines.
155 Car or whatever they got.
156 Meaning you should not ever be competitive.

Stay with a good vibration, by being happy for other people's success, so that neutral—positive things happen to you, too.

The "*Law of Clarity*" states that when you give your vibration a negative thought, you will act and respond in a negative way. So if you want neutral or positive waves, look at everything as if it is good or bad. For example, as sad and horrific as the Holocaust was, it was the required event that led to the creation of the State of Israel. It allowed Jews from around the world to come together and acknowledge their existence as a group. This Jewishness in being a people was lost in history because of assimilation. It is all in how you look and perceive a situation.

Do you see the outcome as a negative or a positive?

No matter how good or bad your life is, it is all up to you. How you look at life can be seen differently by each person. It is up to each of you, to understand and comprehend how powerful your thoughts are. You have the power to choose how to think, this is the "*Law of Love*".

The "*Law of Polarity, Placidity and Rhythm*" are different versions of the same energy, given their higher or lower frequencies. Expression and expansion, moving forward as a person. Good or bad[157] depends on your perception; it is how you think. What you may consider as "*common sense*" may not be to another.

Every situation you look at, you can respond to in different ways. You give it meaning until you label it. Just because there is a recession, that does not mean mean you will be in the same place and situation, personally. Thinking positively helps. You plan ahead in a recession, and attract what you have to offer. People will always buy although

157 These are labels we use as physical beings.

maybe not as much as before, however, I believe in abundance so they will still spend and buy.

The "*Law of Rhythm*" defines that, in nature, there is a pattern, the cycle of nature; patterns in the Universe can be seen as your own cycles in your body. Do not resist your cycle; you will be attracting the "*Universal Law of Creation*", which is the cause to draw near what you ask or wish for.

Ralph Waldo Emerson[158] commented on the Law of Cause and Effect said; "*Every cause has an effect, and every effect has a cause.*" It can also be said that every act has its reward, and energy just **IS**, and it cannot be destroyed.

Every act has its reward, so stop doubting, stop worrying, and stop having fear, for the Universe works in "*order*".

Focus on the cause; let the Universe handle the effect when it is ready. Stay on the right vibrations at all time. Gratitude and love are the highest vibration. Start with gratitude, by being happy the Universe is working in order, and it will send you better results.

Once again, gratitude, together with love, is the greatest and strongest vibrational energy. Now take out your pencil again, and write down all that you are grateful for in your life.

If you are a whiner and complainer, writing down what you are grateful for will make you see that there is nothing really to complain about, so focus on the positive. Even if you feel down, I want you to look at your lists that I have asked you to write throughout this book,

158 This was first spoken of in eastern spiritual karma writings, RWE simply commented that simple men believe in luck, wise men believe in cause and effect.

and "*feed*" yourself the positive frequency you wrote. Build a vision board[159] or treasure chest to follow your goals.

Grateful	Goals
1.	1.
2.	2.
3.	3.
4.	4.
5.	5.
6.	6.
7.	7.
8.	8.
9.	9.
10.	10.

Stay in that higher frequency of happiness without doubt, worry or fear, and focus on the details of when and how the Universe will help you. Use your extrasensory perception towards it, by being enamoured[160] by it.

No matter how many negatives you hear or see in the newspaper, television or radio, choose to select how you want to think and live your life. Deconstruct your former self by not letting everyone's negative thoughts affect your thinking.

My advice to you is to stop watching what may disturb you, lead you into negative thoughts, or take your smile, or happy mood away from you. If you are like me, you can see the positive and continue.

Learn to deconstruct and reconstruct yourself. Manifest a life full of abundance. You will require a replacement idea for that negative

159 Chapter 8: The Vision Board
160 Loved

thought. The Universal Law of Creation is a simple process, so lose your negative barriers by changing your thoughts. Look at things positively even in a negative situation. The True Sense of Power is given to you; these are positive thoughts that "*can*" change your life. Imagine yourself in the **NOW**, not in the future; imagining the inner beauty will get the outer beauty. Focus on the neutral—positive things of life without fear or doubt.

You have to take the Truth of what you know and make it a positive feeling. By seeing only the positive outcome, you become a stronger person.

You are not safe from anything; this is a false illusion. How you deal with it is your choice. Fight negative, and bring it around to a positive. This is a mental workout that takes time to perfect. However, once you reach it, all negativity shall hide or disappear.

You will love it when this happens to you. You will push away those negative people who make fun of you while on your new venture of positive thought.

Manifestations of music[161] are a very good for finding yourself or even finding a relationship. You have to write what you want from a relationship in detail, not what you want in looks, but in qualities.[162] This way the Universe will get your frequency, again, focus on the positive of "*you*" and let the Universe worry about the details in when and where.

You will not know who, how or when, but it will come, "*for you are truly beautiful and worth it*", for beauty is only in the eyes of the

161 Subliminal.
162 Looks should be the last thing on your list. Looks should be the "bonus"

beholder. If you do not find yourself pretty or attractive, then that is what you will attract towards you.

You must shift to powerful neutral—positive thoughts when things become negative. If one person thinks positive, it will hit someone else's thoughts in a network, just as negative energy,[163] all it takes is one person.

What do I want in my life?

Where do I want to be now?

All begins with your "*THOUGHTS*". The fear of doubt feeds you; as a result, you have to get rid of repetitive negative thinking. Do not let someone else's thoughts affect your thoughts, for what is good for someone else, does not mean it is good for you.

What is it that you want from money or a relationship?

Write it down in details.

Do you believe it is as easy to make one million dollars as a dollar?[164]

If not, then pick an amount that feels more real to you. Start small like one hundred dollars, one thousand dollars, or ten thousand dollar and start feeling what it is like to own that much.

When the logical mind pops up, deconstruct and change your perceptions to positive ones, do a reconstruction of it.

163 Violence the Media shows on television or these so call Freedom Fighters spreading anger. As a mass you are creating that reality when you follow and listen to it.
164 See Chapter 3 : Positive Thought

Focus on you so you can empower yourself to see what you truly require and want. By this, you will see that you finally can control your thoughts. Half the battle is knowing how, and the other half is knowing the negative thoughts, for you deserve to be comfortable while enjoying life.

Now you know what you want, as well as you know that the Universe will deal with the details and take your old controlling habit away. The Universal Creator will take care of you. This does not mean you should be laid back and be lazy, but that you must "*work with it*" to see the signs the Universe gave you, so that you can receive it. I do not limit myself when the Universe gives me signs to contact certain people that may help in my advancement, along with theirs.[165]

I trust it, with all my inner being. I enjoy the positive; and as a result I do not see the negative, for I will transform all and any negative into a positive situation.

For every positive thought you have in your mind, there are fifteen negative thoughts you must eliminate, otherwise for every positive thought there are fifteen negative thoughts that enter our mind.[166] Once you finally eliminate your negative thoughts, and run over, in your mind, with positive thoughts, you shall reach your reason of why you are here.

Negative thoughts over run ninety—seven point three percent of the population around the world, while less than two point seven percent of the world population knows this secret. The "*Ones*" and the "*Shadows*" are giving you just a glimpse of the Truth — for you to Truly comprehend this gift that has always been there for you. However, they know that no

165 Investors or people finding me as in Gavriel Navarro (www.gavrielnavarro.com/) and those who are interested in translating my books in different languages.

166 Refer to Chapter 13: Cross Road To Life, Book II: Time Is An Illusion, Chapter 4: The Truth, subtitle "II Receiving Reality" and Book III: Illuminatis The Ones and The Shadows, Chapter 2: Hidden Clues.

matter what positive information we relay to the mass population, the majority of you will be in denial of what is being given.[167]

Negative thoughts will keep you from having what you truly want or even make you lose what you have built. Negative thoughts can make you believe that "*this is too good to be true*", and make you believe you are running on "*luck*" that will run out soon.[168] Positive thoughts run on cause and effect by being "*fortunate*"[169] not being "*lucky*" and that is your birthright for you will have a joyous, prosperous, and grateful life.

Believe in thought patterns, starting in small, repetitive, mental patterns. Delete old negative thinking patterns as you deserve a new start. Trust and see.

Do not micromanage it; let the Universe do it consequently so that you can enjoy the positive energy you now put out. Most people will be thinking on autopilot while you shall no longer be doing it.

"*Master*" your mind to think properly for your world is like a mirror and you become what you think; whatever you put out, you get back. Therefore, if you are lazy and you do not work with the Universe, you will get nothing in return.

It is the "*Ancient Universal Law of Creation*", which has always been there since time began.

There is nothing to give up on for every failure is a stepping stone to success since it may look like you failed ten thousand times but from that you finally succeeded once which is worth more then the combined ten thousand times. I have revised what Thomas Edison said into my own experience.

167 Book II: Time is an Illusion and Book III: Illuminatis The Ones and The Shadows.
168 Wise men believe in "cause and effect".
169 Bringing some good thing not foreseen as certain.

Chapter 12

Extreme Thoughts

"For a man to conquer himself is the first and noblest of all victories."
— **Plato**

If you find yourself in a situation which you consciously don't desire to be in, then remember that somewhere in your subconscious thoughts that place is where you secretly wanted to be, so that you would be forced, with no choice, but to finally wake up.

An extreme example would be finding yourself imprisoned. I personally found being incarcerated a positive experience since it woke me up to who I really am and have always been.[170] I went through a metamorphosis; I had all the time in the world to see myself for who I am, was and who I am not.

I have built contacts and associations with other positive individual people I would not have had the privilege and opportunity to have met or been, interested, in before. I took a negative experience and made it into a positive experience; "*for they can take away my freedom, but they cannot take away my love for life*". I gave hope not only to other

170 Those with the Gift should remember who I Truly AM. I was known by over one hundred different name in the Spiritual Realm (Outer Dimension).

inmates but also to the Correctional Officers who worked there. Some left to pursue other ventures because of my teachings. I have no fear of prison, or to find myself once more there. It was not blind coincidence that brought me there, but a divine plan.

Only you have control of your true thoughts. You have created your situation as it is, and you do have the power to change it. Do not let others' negative thoughts influence you; it is always a choice, a conscious choice. The battle is never over, unless you say so, for you create your own reality to succeed or fail.

I hope that you are finally starting to understand this secret that has been around longer than time itself. A Universal Law that can never be changed. The law is you attract whatever you choose to give your attention to, whether you consciously want to or not. Do you comprehend this?

The pen and mind are the most powerful tools you can use to improve your life.

How is that? You ask.

Writing unleashes a force that is far greater than your actions could ever produce by themselves.[171]

Why?

You write down your thoughts, your goals, and your life experience, even other peoples' thoughts and goals; people you see as successful, who are where you want to be if you have to. It is important to write

171 Your actions can be forgotten, however what is written can give you "immortality" and become more meaningful in time.

every day, however do not worry how to start… just start. Do you follow this concept or not?

If you truly want to change your thought processes, you have to be dedicated to change by implementing everything you read in this book. Otherwise, if you continue to focus on your life's limitations, you will continue to create and attract more limitations into your life. Do you follow me so far?

However, if you instead focus on abundance and prosperity that is already in your presence, even if in reality it is trivial, then you will begin to create, as a result, a more abundance, prosperity and wealth without faking it.[172]

I understand you have a huge obstacle to overcome, barriers that you most likely did not know about or knew even existed.

Do you know what it is?

It is your subconscious block; it has probably been there all your life. All you need is to unblock it.

Only you have the power to transform your life to what you want it to be forever. Money is not your answer nor will it make you happy, it will only make you worry how long it will be there before it is all gone. Am I right?

Yet if you consistently think and feel wealthy every moment of every day and night, you will stay or become wealthy. You see the big different?

172 Refer to Jake Hollow's "The Jake Hollow Guide on How to Persuade Women" Social Engagements Chapter 4: With Women, Chapter 15: Positive Thinking, and Jake Hollow's "How to Deal with Emotions and the Life of a Motivational Speaker" Part II: Defining Emotions Chapter 4: Words Can Lie, the Body Cannot.

Have you ever wondered why when somebody has won millions of dollars then a few years later they find themselves back to being poorer than before?

How about Millionaires and Billionaires who have gone bankrupt, yet somehow still found a way a few years later to become wealthy and, in addition, more powerful than before?

That is, the second has a mindset in abundance while the other does not. So my question to you is;

Where is your mindset?

You can make up whatever excuses you want, however the Truth is inside of you.

You get to use your imagination, and make things up, daydream, or pretend. In the end, you get to fake[173] your reality until you make it. Only you can create whatever it is you desire in your life.

Bear in mind that the Universe has something in store for you; in addition all you are required to do is see it, and be aware of it.

When you have a thought, or speak a word, the energy you created vibrates and goes out. As a result it attracts "*like*" vibrational energy and brings results back to your reality.

Quantum physics has proven that everything in the Universe is vibrating. To better understand this concept, take for example the frequency waves of your radio, television, or internet; these are waves

173 This does not mean to "Pretend". You must truly believe and be convinced that it is there already.

but then this energy is transformed into content. It attracts back what you want.

Therefore, as I have written before, if your mind and thought is set on "*I lack*" or "*I'm limited*", this is the signal you are sending out.

Then you wonder why your life is always the same all the time and it does not improve. If you desire a life of happiness with the purpose of abundance in wealth, you have to change how you think at all times.

The first step in achieving these goals is changing the way you think. Think like a compassionate Billionaire, and you will be one.

Make an effort to understand the concept that everything that comes into a physical reality was first formless; it was actually floating all around you, yet not solid enough that you saw it. You can tap into this formless substance through your heart and mind. This is how you can place the order in what you want. Holding onto an ideal in your heart and mind shall cause it to appear in your physical reality.

You see the problem is that, all too often, you are thinking of what you do not want, which as a result causes the things you do not want to actually happen. Then you wonder why things have not change for you year after year. Change your thoughts; in the end you will change your world!

If you're broke right now, it's because you are thinking more about being broke; not over living a life full of financial freedom. In case you have no idea why you have no money at the moment, it is because you are thinking more about having no money than over being wealthy.

Therefore, as a result of your thinking, your thoughts expand into feelings.

You become emotionally and physically down because of the thought that you do not have enough. This continues to create that life of not having enough. You are re—creating that same life over and over again. Only you can change the way you think by looking at it the way you want it to be, and not the way you do not want. Seeing yourself wealthy.

Benjamin "*Bugsy*" Siegel[174] was a visionary and saw the lights of Vegas before anything was built in the desert. People believed he was nuts. He believed what he imagined, however he died before he could see it.

Dreams are reality, they float in the air. You just require believing and ordering them for them to become solid.

It is easier to come up with excuses why you cannot achieve your goals, which will hold you back from living out your dreams. You can manifest what you attract when you are patient and believe without a doubt you shall achieve it. It is not required for you to know the details of how you will achieve your goal. All you must do is go deep inside yourself and see what you would love to see happen in your life.

Be clear and specific in what you want, start small before you go to bigger things, for you do not want to feel it is an impossible goal.

You have absolutely no idea how many times your desires are in and out. What I mean by this is, that one moment you are full of life and believe you can achieve it, then later on you build doubt along with lack of confidence. **DO NOT CONFUSE THE UNIVERSE!**

174 Siegel is widely acclaimed as the man who built Las Vegas. His hotel The Flamingo was the first super hotel to be built on the now famous strip, then just a dirt track outside Las Vegas. Jewish gangster Bugsy Siegel, with help from friend and fellow mob boss Meyer Lansky poured money through Mormon owned banks for cover of legitimacy and built The Flamingo in 1946.

I. Is This Gold?

You are supposed to enjoy life; you are here for a reason. It is all in how you condition your thinking process. This means that when you perceive things with a negative perspective, you have to find a way to turn them into a positive view. This is because how you think and react to something affects how you deal with it.

The "*Law of Love*" is the gold the Universe gives to you. If you put love out there, love will be returned; even if you do not know when or how it will show up.

The Universe takes care of the details, the order and timing, from point "*A*" to point "*B*," all the way to point "Z".

Always keep your mind in order with the Universe. Release all fears and doubts by staying in a perfect Universal order. Banish all negative thoughts from your mind, whatever they are, beyond the shadow—of—a—doubt. Always keep yourself in tune with the positive higher vibrations you are on and, in addition, always have perfect faith.

When the Universe sees and feels that you are full of joy, and grateful for what you have, the moment it feels your good vibrations, it will send you more good things. Nevertheless, if it should feel that you are complaining, it will give you more to complain about. My advice to you is to always feel gratefully happy so that the Universe will give you nothing other than happiness.

Feeling is the trigger that the Universe senses and feels. Now out loud yell; "*IS IT NOT NICE …*" then fill in the blank with a positive thought,[175] something that you would like. Picture it clearly in your mind and steadily hold on to that image you want until it becomes a

175 Remark.

definite thought form. Do these one to three times a day and everyday add a new blank spot. On average, you think around sixty thousand thoughts a day in addition ninety percent of these are repetitive. If most of it is on poverty consciousness then;

Is it any wonder you stay in the same place year after year?[176]

The answer is to switch your thoughts to a prosperity consciousness, by making it your predominant focus. Do not ever sabotage this with doubt.[177]

Never get too wrapped up in emotions when you are working on achieving a certain goal. Learn to deal with things without using your emotions. Build your objective goals without emotions, and let the Universe worry about the details in helping you achieve your success and let your dreams becoming a reality. You now have an edge, as this knowledge is gold.

Your particular "*vision*" of what you want is very important. Make a "*commitment*" to yourself and your future by thinking in the **NOW**.

Your vision is more important than your goal. Commitment, is very important as well. If you just think "*I believe I have a mission*", then you will "*never*" receive what you truly want.[178] It must all be done in obedience to the Law by which the Universe was created. Do not violate this "*Ancient Law*", for it is absolute. So once again, write that list so you do not lose track of your mission that you committed yourself to.

Build your self—esteem with your self—respect by having self—confidence always in a higher frequency.

176 This is not just financially, but emotionally in relationship and any others misery you are facing on a regular basis.
177 Refer to The Jake Hollow Guide on How to Persuade Women "Social Engagements"
178 Not acting on it with an action.

Chapter 13

Cross Road to Life

"I decided that it was not wisdom that enabled poets to write their poetry, but a kind of instinct or inspiration, such as you find in seers and prophets who deliver all their sublime messages without knowing in the least what they mean." — **Socrates**

I love the prefect way of achieving the goal that I envision. It is a feeling of being able to create. To create is perfection, at its best. The same way a reaction is to a given action; so an action is to a reaction.

Time is peripheral since once time goes, it is gone.
Time is indispensable; it is the act to react.
Time is irreplaceable, without interruption.

Time is the goal to commit to a promise of what you want and will achieve. Money is not, but you can get it in time.

Learn to retract your time by receiving. In about two to three months from that moment, you will start to believe in this and change. Just live love. For example, the more you spend your time with loved ones,[179] the more you feel their love together along with your love to them. '*Time*' has the same concept.

Once you become aware of a "*thought*", you become like a child when time seemed slower and you were only in the moment without thought. So, you must practice, as well as, re—master this in a natural way by not relying on thought and being in the **NOW** moment. You create what your life is as well as how it is going to be. Learn to be in the eternal **NOW** and not to think of the past or the so—called future with fear, worry and stress.[180]

The moment is what you know, so do not feed the so called past or future when the past is gone and the future has not even happened. When you fear the future, your fear creates a potential future that has not even happened — you may even predict that things will go wrong. This becomes a self—fulfilling prophecy. You are too worried to relax or balance your life to see the clearer path. Stop projecting the worst.

This is an opportunity to have a better life by being in the **NOW** moment with an awareness of all. For example, if I asked you to focus on your breathing and, instead you are worrying about how busy you are or that you have more problems than others to even bother with trying. Thinking this way, in reality, causes you to rush time and live an unhappy life.

What I give to you has nothing to do with me; this information is a gift to help you manage your life better. Whatever has called me, or whomever you can come up with in your own conclusion is a mystery.[181]

179 For me it would be my children.

180 Refer to Jake Hollow's "How to Deal with Emotions and the Life of a Motivational Speaker" Part II: Defining Emotions Chapter 4: Anger, Fear, Stress, and Worry.

181 Whatever belief you may have as in religious or scientifically.

When you make a mistake in the moment, which can also be called **NOW**,[182] we do not worry as if we made a mistake in the thinking timeline where you are stressed with worries.[183] The Universal Truth is to evolve so, when you evolve, you can control time or devolve by letting time take over. Learn to master the ability to always be in the **NOW** moment. Master expanding your mind, your being. Self—improvement or education is true human nature. Bringing joy is the key and this is something most people do not do. Once you truly focus, you will see that the problem you believe to be real is but an illusion you created.

When you face a challenge, focus and write it down. Somewhere on that list, you will find the solution and this will empower you. Always take a deep breath and relax while staying focused on your breathing.

I live in the **NOW** moment and only think in the moment. This is why I never worry or become stressed because time and space are one. It takes discipline, and discipline has gotten me here.

How will you improve yourself if you are looking at others because you feel they are doing better than you are?

Let it go and be yourself in the moment of **YOU**. Be grateful for where you are, together with becoming who you truly are in the **NOW**, by creating the real you.

Always remember that if you have a question to ask, but do not because you feel it is a stupid question, you are wrong. There are no stupid questions even if you feel that your question does not make sense. Your doubt creates what you believe, for whatever you think, will come back to you. Most people choose not to see nor understand

182 Or the present moment.
183 In the Spiritual Realm or as a Spiritual Guru we do not worry or become stressed.

what is written here. These people will say that people like me live in a dream world.

Why are you here?

To learn and better yourself.[184]

Thomas Alva Edison once said; "*I have not failed ten thousand times, I have successfully found ten thousand ways that didn't work*". This is learning by taking a negative situation and turning it into a positive one. You are not a failure until you quit. Only when you quit do you become a failure. Most people do not look for opportunities to enhance themselves to see positive changes. I can only help you if you help yourself, as only you can help yourself if you focus on your true self in the moment. Happiness only comes from within.

To have purpose, you must gain awareness and knowledge by not cheating and by staying on track. Those of you who are successful are so by keeping yourself on track without fear, stress, or worry. Purpose is self—knowledge by connecting with within. You must not disconnect yourself from your life force.

Caring for others should be first while money is second. What is important is caring for others, by thinking of people first before material wealth. This richness is a better than anything else.

The "*intention*" is more important then how you do it. The abundance becomes more enjoyable in this empowerment. You each choose or have chosen to be here as a physical being.

Once you know beyond any shadow—of—a—doubt who you are, you will find true joy in why you are here. I live in honour to serve and

184 You are here on vacation so that Your Higher—Self gains Knowledge.

help others. If you set a goal of, "*I want to get it*", then this comes from your ego. If you set your vision "*to get what you want to help others*", then it is not your selfish ego. It is all about the work. Create Spiritual understanding by living in a place of peace and divinity.

Determine your purpose.
Determine your center of focus.
Determine who you want to help.
Determine what fulfilment (or cd use) "*result*" you want for them.

By living a joyful and purposeful life, where your life is about helping others, you will live a life full of purpose, joy, success, health, and wealth.

You are not a luxury vehicle; you are a person of value. Fundamentally, knowing who you are at your core, as an individual identity, makes the difference. When you express your divine nature and tap into your divine wisdom, you can see yourself in service to others. You project that divine energy into the world.

I have learned to become a vehicle to relay these messages. Therefore, when I write them down, I know it is not from me, but from a Higher Source, that is unknown. You grow in awareness and sense from each other's energy you send. For me to accomplish my goals in vision, I want to help you accomplish yours. When you do this, you help each other by not failing. You help each other get back on your feet. You are not greedy.

I have learned to master being at the right place at the right time.[185] My vision is to find sponsors who will help me build a resort where people can come to gain awareness about empowering themselves. My

185 In the past, this was the case, as well, but I did not pay much attention to the meaning of that and because of that I have lost precious opportunities.

main interest is to be able to make a difference in other peoples' lives by having the time, as well as the funds available to make it happen. [186] My reputation is more important than money.[187] There is no right or wrong reason why you want to make money. The Universe wants you to be successful and rich. That is all that matters!

Whatever you think you will manifest into reality, will be. It works on both the positive and negative vibrations you send out. Therefore, it is up to you to change how you think. It is all in how your mind targets what you're about. Your thought has been around from generation to generation. As this is the case, you require deconstructing so that you can reconstruct how you think.

This will not change over night, my friends. Your subconscious, as well as your inner conscious mind will fight this change because it is accustomed to this safe way you believed was real.

Once you master and learn this, it will take a few months to deconstruct your old thoughts into rebuilding an ancient thought of being connected with the Universe. You will finally see the difference and you will love where you will be. Once you let go of your "*block*", you will see a change in your life. No one can fill your place, but you. Living and giving service to humanity should be your first goal. By serving through this goal, it will give you "*Spiritual abundance*". in this place of divine alignment, the pathway is clear and unclouded.

I thought I created those words from a dream I've received in 2008 but found out in 2011 that these same words came from "Teihard de Chadin" 1881-1955. You are wired to love as well as to take care of others.

186 This is not a scam. I am not about money for the sake of making money or taking yours.
187 I'm not focused on money. Meaning if I achieve in abundance of wealth or not is not important. However my reputation and credibility is my focus.

Learn to drop your doubt and transform it to trust, full trust. Ask for what you want, not who you want. The frequency you bring out will look for its match to bring back to you. Trust it with all your being. Believe in what you want to believe, by shifting your thoughts from what you do not want, to what you do want. Otherwise, ignore and shift the negative things by only focusing on the positive things.

Positive things will come into your life if you let them. Change your focus and more good things will come into your life. Make a difference in your life, my friends. Live your life to the fullest and learn the balance of it. Create well—being in which you will replace negative thought for that positive emerging thought. As I mentioned before, safety is the illusion of the logical mind, while the "*Universal Law of Creation*" is a simple concept that most people do not fully understand. They do not know how to use it and it is taken for granted. Changing your own thoughts starts right now, with your sense of well being and true power, which was given to you at birth.

Let the Universe take care of the "*hows*", so that you can focus on your beautiful traits. To help you, visualize the quality of someone else's traits rather than your own. Focus on the positive or neutral of life with balance, because the Universe will match you up with the right frequency. Therefore, stay focused on your positive traits and know that there is somebody out there looking for you, just like you are looking for them. Banish or change those doubts for trust.

On the economy segment, it is all in how you perceive or believe it is. If you see or hear that we are in a recession and your thought believes this, then this is how you will live your life. You create your own surroundings, so only you can change what's in your personal space. Cause the recession to not affect you by not having fear, worry, and stress, by not accepting the outside way of thinking, and by keeping the perception in how you see things in a positive way rather than in a negative way.[188]

What do you want in or out of your life right NOW?

Make it into a positive thought in every aspect of your life. Do it for health, prosperity, relationships, and happiness. Do not take someone else's opinion even if it is true for others. It may be true for them but it does not mean it is true for you; we are all individuals. Most people feed off doubt and fear and this affects their perception and the way they have lived. Stop letting others' perception of you affect you.

Opinions of others come from their life experience. You can learn from this. Again my question to you is;

What is it that you want in life?

What is it that you want from money?

Go to the real source, go deeper.

Why do you want money?

Write down the answer, it starts with;

Need for security.
Comfort.
Travel.
Etcetera.

If the logical mind brings a negative thought, look at the source. Focus on what it feels like to have money. Write your perception of

188 We all spend to much time analyzing...let us simplify.

money. Money is not the root of all—evil; it is how you use it that can be evil.[189]

For example, I personally do not think of money. I focus more on being healthy, living in prosperity with all beings, being in great relationship with all beings, and having happiness in my life with all of you.

Do not blame your parents when you hear their voice, just deconstruct any negative thought. You do not require those thoughts anymore, you can change those perceptions.

Delete them and change them into the opposite. You require a replacement thought for that emerging thought. Trust the Universe and it will give back to you; just avoid the doubt.

The Universe has been running this world forever, so let go and enjoy life. Be at ease; let it go while looking at the positive of any situation. Just be grateful for everything you have.

In your life you require tools that hold value for you. When you focus on the positive, love will not only be in you but also in those around you. See the true perception of your requirements and desires, so write them down in detail.

Look for the source of positive thinking. Be fair and unbiased without allowing interruptions, feelings of duress, or being stubborn. Work on staying persistent by trusting the Universe to give you what you require; the Universe has already calculated the right moment.

189 The story of Job in the Holy Scripture made it clear that Job was the richest man in the land and then, in the end, with all his suffering, he was rewarded with three times more then he had. It would be like Bill Gates being three times richer than he is now.

Let the Universe worry when it will send it to you. Do not micro—manage how or when you will receive nor what you want or what you will do with it. Please do not misinterpret this with not working for what you want.

Be grateful for what you have and do not worry about how much it will cost you financially.

Most do not fully understand how life works. Once you comprehend how the Universe works, you will see you can and you will create how you live your life, for it is a Universal Law.

How life works is in your own belief system, viewpoints, philosophy, and your inner and outer perspectives. How excited do you feel about it?

You are the Creator of your life; demand to find the Creator within it. You will build a personal awareness of your surroundings, once you form a central idea or concept of yourself, by tapping your principle of power.

The moment you fully understand these ideas, you will be able to transform your life by transforming your thoughts.

You absolutely have to learn to master how to handle your negative emotions, energy, and thoughts, before you can turn them into anything positive. The whole process is very important. What the Ancient Secret is about is how to apply this using the Universal Law in a proper way.

Most people are not patient and expect years and years of their negative upbringing to be eliminated in a day. On the contrary, it takes work to reconstruct your own thinking process to a newer, more

Spiritual way of positive happy thoughts. It is all in your attitude and how you master it.

Vision starts in your mind; this you create from a single seed. Nothing is created from thin air. You become what you think. Your vision is grounded in positively. Now ask yourself;

What is it that I am passionate about?

Use your mind and build a vision, close your eyes, focus on your breathing while slowly building a vision in your mind. Your vision has to be in alignment with your values.

Whatever you do, do not struggle, just let it flow. If you are struggling with your vision, it could be your lack of self—confidence or that your heart is not in it.

What is the next value, beyond love, honesty, and integrity that you value the most?

Your lover makes you think about the use of your time, and how to profit from it. We all have a Cosmic connection with each other and with the energy of the Cosmos. You are powerful with all beings and energy. Considering this: you feel no guilt, worry or stress with no expectation.

You live in cycles; you see it in nature itself. That is why you must defend your position against your problems. When you face a challenge, write it down so that you come up with solutions. Having fear or discouragement cripples you when you do not reach for information that can enhance your life. Start embracing knowledge and you will start to make positive changes from your discomfort.

Innerfective[190] therapy offers an alternative to issues on motivation, communication skills, and self awareness.

The desire to change yourself and your relationships has to be there. When there are conflicts between two people, you should look and examine yourself.

Find the truth about who you are without being defensive. When you are on the defensive, you give away your power. So, if anybody criticizes you, work on finding the Truth about being criticized.

If you continue to go on the defensive, they will continue criticizing you so stop being defensive. You are second guessing yourself, and you will let someone else define your reality. Working to manipulate the way they see things empowers them.

You create what you feel or want while the mass population believes you should feel and think like them. This is like acting like sheep, while believing they have free will.

You have to identify and recognize the negative around you. If you want to recognize the positive around you, you have to overtake the negative, until it sees it no longer influence you, you being the so called "*ego*". You want to dig deep, in ways you can empower yourself.

I have learned to be enlightened and inspired by knowledge. Teaching has made the difference and has become a passion that I now see clearly. Before, I missed the greatest Truth ever communicated to humankind. I was not about to repeat that same mistake.

Once you understand that you can identify with it, then you can ask yourself;

190 Inside (inner self) your belief system.

Is my belief invalid?

Positive thinking is not easy but it is a workout that you must do. All can say they are positive, just because on the outside they seem to be, but are they?

To receive an abundance of all good things, you will need to erase all negative that is inside and around you and then replace it with positive thoughts.

I know I keep repeating this over and over. The fact is that this is my way of ensuring you do not forget. You must fully comprehend that for every fifteen negatives you eliminate, and you will replace them with one positive.[191]

The Law of the Universe is not to give out of guilt for you are selling yourself out. You give because you do not expect anything in return. Negative is a physical illusion you created from your thoughts.

You become what you think. Some of you may even ask;

Why are others in a better situation than me in health, wealth, and relationships?

My answer to you is; "*you must have not taken care of your health, you didn't manage your money correctly, and you didn't listen closely to your relationship*".

It all has to do with how you think and that you "*must take full responsibility for your actions and thoughts*". The moment you "*stop blaming*" and take full "*responsibility*", is the moment you reconstruct

191 Refer to Chapter 11: Passion Should Be Your Goal and Book II: Time Is an Illusion, Chapter 4: The Truth, subtitle "II Receiving Reality"

your thoughts to a positive aftermath leading to a better relationship, health or wealth.

Now do not ask yourself;

What is holding me back?[192]

Ask instead;

What is holding me from going forward?[193]

Do you see the difference between these two questions?

One is a problem, while the other is a solution. So get rid of all excuses, and become who you really truly are to those loved ones who will be proud of you.[194] When you seek and ask, you shall receive. When you receive it, you will find joy and happiness. This is genuine.

Whatever you think, it will come back to you. Magical thinking is how it happens.

An advertiser uses a vision board to catch people's minds; it is the same with using your thoughts in visions so that the Universe can receive your frequency and as a result it sends back to you what you want and not the opposite.

You never have to worry about being on your own. You are never alone; the Universe is always with you.

The Truth has been hidden for milleniums from our Secret Ancestors who changed how we used our thoughts. Your thought

192 Past.
193 Future NOW.
194 As well as you shall be proud of yourself, even without anyone there to cheer you.

has been changed to the illusion you now see, which is not real, yet you cannot hide it forever. You are now given a new chance to use your thoughts as they were originally meant to be used and have always been.

You must be truly grateful and happy in all your being so that the Universe gets the right frequency. Failure is a gateway through which you must temporarily pass in order to access your deeper core.

CHAPTER 14

Master Your Belief

"Don't let anything stand in the way of you claiming and manifesting the life that you choose rather than the life you have by default."
— Joy Page

There are times when I am asked a question to which everyone expects me to give a profound answer. However, my experience has taught me to answer certain questions with another question, making the room come alive. This always wakes everyone up and educates them towards a greater understanding.

You will rebuild your world; you will reconstruct, reorganize, and enjoy the greatest prosperity, as well as, the most wonderful life. You will all work for a common goal.

Learn to master your mind and soul, so you can take control of your life. Take this challenge, for everyone loves a challenge. First, you have to know where you want to go or who you want to become. Have a guide and a deadline as these are important. If you cannot figure out what is holding you back, it is most likely that you have low self— confidence and self—esteem, or else you would have figured it out.

Once you see and recognize the downside, we can help you spot the upside. This way you can see and acknowledge what's holding you from going forward and focus on it.

You must ask yourself;

What kind of help do I want?

Is it more of a guideline, a relax session in trancing, or meditation?

First. What is my value and commitment?

Look at the root cause, fully understand your personal value and the fact that your commitment is a promise you must keep for the sake of your integrity. Do whatever you have to… to keep your commitment and yourself on track. If you want to move forward, inspire yourself, have fun, and do not take life too seriously.

The Universal Laws govern everything. Unlimited things are there for you with unlimited possibilities. If you work with the Universe and put your things in motion, you will not struggle in a unified field of infinitive possibilities.

Most of you know that everything is energy, so if you look at yourself;

Is your energy vibrating at a high frequency or at a low frequency in living out your dream?

If you run away from your problem;

What are you saying about yourself?

Part of being an energy being is finding happiness, however to find it you must first find true passion in life, in your self—worth.

If life kicks you down, it is because deep down, it is what you want. It is your job to plan a stronger strategy with no false notions and get back up. When one door closes, another one opens. All you must do is profess the courage to enter it with a real intention, while believing in yourself by not suppressing your fears. If you do suppress them, the energy will be expressed somewhere else. So let it go and allow it to go. When people blame, they are looking for excuses outside of themselves, they want to look at another source.

Know who you are, know your value, and know your passions. These are unlimited. No matter how hard you look, it is right in front of you — it always has been there.

Once you show gratitude, true gratitude, it will become a part of your being. It will be within you, not out of you. You will receive unlimited possibilities.

So, if you are serious about changing your life, then make a true commitment to your desire and take full responsibility by not blaming others or blaming yourself. Believe in who you are.

If you are in a conversation with someone and you notice that they do not want to listen to you,[195] it is because they are consumed with themselves.[196] They are afraid since what you may be saying could be happening to them.

Everything relates to energy.

195 You are talking about great news you are going through or giving good advice.

196 They are focused on their ego. If you were negative by complaining that would be another issue.

Is this situation increasing your energy levels to heighten and take responsibility for yourself?

You, as I, have an assignment to pursue. Allow yours to take over, and interesting things will happen. Success comes from the heart; it's your power source.

Live in unlimited possibilities. Acknowledging them, then allowing them to manifest into reality. Success is everywhere; you are success. As people get interested, they participate in your own reproduction. What you can hold in your mind and heart, you can hold in your hand.

Certain people will have problems sending the right frequency to the Universe, while others will not.

It's all in how much you believe and trust, while fully comprehending the concept that the Universe will accept your frequency and provide your wish at the right moment, when you least expect it to reach you.

If you cannot comprehend this, then you are working against the Universe. You become the cancer cell in the Universal body.

If you are not doing something according to your values, then deep inside you, you did not change your belief system. This does not happen overnight. Question those belief systems because these challenges can bring you great opportunities in your life. Treat these relationships as precious gifts in your life; start treating them that way. Now, yell from the top of your lungs;

I'M SO HAPPY AND GRATEFUL BECAUSE ...

Add what you feel.

Work on changing your mindset, take responsibility, and do not blame others or yourself. Start planning your life and believe in yourself. Let go of the "*how's*" and "*why's*"; use your thoughts as seeds.

You have to use your thoughts as when you plant a seed: one at a time, in the ground to fertilize ovules[197] capable of developing into a new source of beginning, not just your mind.

You have been disconnected from your Spirit far too long for the Universe to understand your frequency clearly.

Your goal is to re—find your Spiritual and physical—self connection before they were separated millenniums upon millenniums ago, so that as you visualize in your mind, you can send out your Spiritual thoughts as seeds. You all know that a seed requires nurturing and watering before it sprouts. The Universe works the same way. So imagine that, in the physical plane, the Universe is the soil and the thought frequency you are sending is the seed you will plant in the soil.

Depending if each seed planted was planted in the right or wrong way, the seeds will grow into whatever you wanted them to grow. So, the Universe will send back what you planted to you. If you were lazy and didn't plant the seed correctly or took care of the plant, then you went against the Universe. If you did it right, with tender loving care, the Universe will send back what you desired in your wish. It will be delivered to you at the moment it is fully grown and at the right time when you least expected. You may have even forgotten how beautiful it is and how surprised you would be.

Form follows thought. You were designed to create, so use your thoughts as seeds and plant them correctly. Start slowly from the bottom, not the top. Let go of what you think you require or want.

197 A small egg; especially: one in an early stage of growth.

Recognize opportunities and act on them. You require only to listen and understand how to work with the energy. As seeds of creation, it requires a root system, creating from the bottom up in three dimensions. So, let go of what you want, for the Universe is listening to the big thing.[198]

Learn to go on your journey while letting go of all worries for the Universe will watch over you with your Spiritual Guide beside you. You only manifest how you feel in the moment.

If you are worried, you are focusing on the future.[199] If you want to manifest good things, you must absolutely focus on the present. I call this my Eternal **NOW**.

When you are worried, you are focused on a future that has not happened. Get away from being scared; just go on the journey and process to unblock what is stopping you. Getting to the root of the matter is the single step for you to do. When you are worried, you are creating a negative future where you completely miss the moment of **NOW**. The Universe is going to bring you what you want, so no need to be afraid. You can live anywhere. It knows who you are so go on this journey, wherever it goes.

Worries equals a probable disappointing future

You know you are energy that you can create by manifesting. Therefore, if you use your mind to focus on an automobile vehicle you want, you cannot just visualize it; on the contrary, you create this infinite possibility from scratch by building it with details. You are starting it as a seed and slowly building it one—step at a time. Unblock your thoughts to a clearer view of vision.

198 Subtitle Chapter 17: Obligation, subtitle "I Self—Taught"
199 A future that has not even happen.

Picture in your mind where, what, and how you want something and the Universe will react from all the details you want.

You must pay close attention to your surroundings. Hidden clues are all around you to lead you to where you should go. Start with relaxation, and meditate by first focusing on your breathing, then once you feel relaxed, build and create your thoughts as if they are in front of you, step by step.

Do not make it just appear out of thin air instantly, but build it piece by piece, and then send it out to the Universe in the order you selected, just as you would from the internet or a catalogue. Let it flow out so that you can then receive it. It is vital to work with energy and not against it.

As a Visionary, you ensure that the entity always remains aligned with its long—term objectives. As the builder implements the vision, it directs the mechanics of operation towards its intended goals. To visualize something without building is aimless.

To understand energy, let me use an explanation.

Have you ever… that you just did not like someone or even felt uncomfortable with them for no apparent reason?

However, you have never even talked to, or met, so;

Why?

Well, that is your energy vibration at a certain frequency letting you know they are not compatible. It can be for many reasons, as in being past lives enemies or in the not so distant future, they will betray you.

Do not just visualize it for it to manifest itself, but integrate the affirmation as one in singularity. Once you truly get it, by seeing the connection, you will see and feel the change you want. Fear stops you from moving forward.

If deep inside you feel you have negative energy, look at how you can re—create yourself and the way you think. My father (bless his soul) told me in Italian; "*Se si associa con i porco, diventerai un porco*".[200] My father was a disturbed man, but wise nonetheless. Poverty consciousness leads to fear, so that when you strive at manifesting negatively, it shows you do not believe you have the right to create. Unblock yourself from these negative feelings and ground your wisdom to sustain you. Accept that you have this negative way of thinking and that you are ready to break away from it finally. Embrace the fears by facing your fears, and let it touch you so that you will not be afraid. Then when you become the fear, you will not fear it anymore.

I'm a strong person, some call me a "*Lion*". I bring my energy down to my feet, to the ground that I feel, then out to the Universe, Multiverse and Outer Dimension. It's a beautiful expansion. Here I feel all the energy that will manifest will make things happen even quicker. Pay attention to your feet and look down to them while you visualize you are where you want to be. Grounded.[201]

Get out of fear;

What is blocking you?

Go to the root of the problem.

Next thing is to manifest in the present moment.

200 If you associate with pigs, you will become a pig.
201 Refer to Chapter 18: Take Your Time, subtitle "II Undesirable Matters"

I. Heart Shape

THE UNIVERSE KNOWS EVERYTHING ABOUT you, and will bring to you, either what matches you, or even better than what you may expect. You cannot just dream yourself to what you want; you have to work on it, for the Universe puts the possibilities in front of you, while it is your job to notice it and do something about it.

If it is of interest to someone, you must make sure that both of you are in the same frequency so you can match. If you put things in motion, there will be no struggle. When you find the thing you should be doing, then, that is when you shall know where you belong.

While I was incarcerated, a friend[202] flicked a rubber band at me; it hit my neck on the left side. Some of the inmates and Correctional Officers came up to me, asking why I had a "*heart shape*" with an "*arrow*" going through it on my neck. I took that as a sign that someone was thinking of me in a romantic or loving way, and it manifested on my neck as a clue.

When people see that these beliefs work for you, people will gather and follow you.[203] This will become repetitive. Those who do not believe or feel it was just pure luck will stay in the same situation they are in.

Most people focus on the idea that the world will make you happy, but reality is that only you can make yourself happy. Good things come without questioning the Universal Laws, as long as you truly trust it to be. Humankind says you can't trust, while I tell you aloud: "*TRUST THE UNIVERSE WITH ALL YOUR BEING WITHOUT ANY DOUBT WHATSOEVER, FOR IT WILL MANIFEST ITSELF IF YOU WAKE UP AND SEE THE SIGNS!*"

202 Big Worm (end of March 2009).
203 This following is more in being inspired by you, without putting you on a pedestal.

The Universe is clear on the fact that its desires are for you to have everything you want. Once you know how to plant those lavish seeds, you can create as much as you wish. Suspend disbelief and scepticism; take certain actions by writing down your commitment and goals with affirmations so that you can run them over and over in your mind until you no longer have negative thoughts only positive. This shall transform your future, your life. Work without action will not give you results.

As I have written earlier. I have been looking deeper into why there are certain people who not only know how to make money but also how to use it and hold on to it all, while others just seems to lose it.

Have you ever pondered over this?

You see, the source is that it all has to do with how you think of financial wealth, it is that simple. The moment you declare; "*I don't have any money*", you are silently stating that whenever you are around any amount of money, high or low, you just seem to blow it. Do you see where I am going with this, before you continue reading?

The same can be applied to a physical relationship.

The Universe gets your call and as a result makes certain that not only will you never be financially wealthy or in a great relationship, when you do make a lot of money or find that right person to fulfill your life, it will all disappear faster than you can keep it.[204]

You have to fully accept that deep down inside, your real emotional fear has never been "*about*" having money, a romantic relationship, or being financially secure and secure in a relationship. It has always been

204 To the Universe the concept of what is right or wrong, good or bad does not exist. The Universe does not judge. The Universe deals in logic and not emotions as we humans do. It only follows our deepest hidden thoughts.

about "*not*" having money and "*not*" having a long term relationship. You secretly feel it is not your birthright.

Do you see the difference in these two meanings?

Your dominant thoughts are vibrating that order to the Universe twenty—four hours a day, day after day, and night after night. The Universe has been giving you just what you wanted, which is your true fears, your true desires, and your true demands.

What is it?

For you to have "*NO MONEY!*" The same goes for a serious relationship and anything else, in general.

Everything that happens, happens for a reason. The people that betray you is to help you get back on track. To get back on track you must learn to forgive and let go.

There is nothing to give up. Every failure is a stepping stone to success since it may look as if I failed ten thousand times, that I finally succeeded in one. Revised what Thomas Edison said into my own expression.

CHAPTER 15

Do You Quit?

"Once you learn to quit, it becomes a habit." — **Vince Lombardi**

At onetime, our Ancient Ancestors lived longer because of their awareness of thoughts. They were in tune with creating and they were a think tank. If today you had a quarter of the knowledge our Ancient Ancestors had in regard to focusing their wishing thoughts together, we would be a force to be reckoned with. If more than one mind is put together with one thought to create with heart and mind, combined it will result with unlimited possibilities.[205]

Shifting your mental attitude and deepening your passions are key. When your energy is positive, everyone will pick up on it. You are effected by your surroundings. Surrender your fears and worries, so that you may see a clearer path. Accept your fears by not suppressing them, but by showing them and then releasing them in a positive way.

When you express yourself, you become a collective energy with those who want to listen. Those who do not want to listen don't because

205 Refer to "Book III: Illuminatis The Ones and The Shadows"

they are too consumed with their own problems; it is not because they do not want to listen.

Everything you do is related to energy. So you must ask;

Will my state of being raise my energy or will it lower it?

In my belief system, I want to keep my energy frequency on a high positive.

If you follow other peoples' values, then you do not know who you are. Discover your inner values', these represent what you are worth and once you know the answer to this, you will have made a step towards to knowing yourself. When you are down, get back right up, for when one door closes, another one opens. All you must do is profess the courage to move through the door.

There is no such thing as accidents, everything happens for a reason that leads to something that will affect your outcome. When this happens in your life, it is an opportunity for you to notice and take advantage of it. Sometimes you may fall deep, however;

Do you quit or get back up?

Once you find what you truly love with deep, true passion, you will show your purpose and will not quit. You will follow your commitment to your mission. This will make you stronger, not only in body, but also in wisdom and knowledge.

So trip! Do not quit! You may break or you might become stronger, it is up to you and no one else. Persistence shows determination. Nothing in the physical world happens over night, just take one—step at a time and at the same time, value your life with gratitude.

To change to the life you desire, you must first change your mind set. Invest moderately in yourself, by first accepting your faults; then, stop blaming yourself or others for not being happy in your life. Build your self—respect, self—worth, and your self—confidence.

The time is near when both reality and unreality will merge once again into two new realities.[206]

I. Question Yourself Seriously

The fastest way to change your life into what you want is to first change how you think life works. Do you agree?

Is your reality focus working for you?

I am sure it is not or else you would not have chosen this book. You have become a sheep in the system.

So what would be the logical answer?

STOP! Stop focusing on what you do not want, and what you believe is impossible.

JUST STOP! You and only **YOU** are creating that reality. I will say this repeatedly throughout my book until my teaching is ingrained deep, deep into your inner core. *YOU ARE CREATING THE REALITY YOU ARE LIVING NOW!*

206 Refer to Book III: Illuminatis The Ones and The Shadows "Chapter 12: Only a Flash", subtitle "I BeginningEnd"

From the beginning of my book I've asked you, my readers, to answer every, and I do mean "*EVERY*" question you've read or will read and write down an answer, "*yes*" or "*no*"?

Now, have you done as instructed?

I would anticipate that over eighty percent of you have not. You are most likely talkers not doers. Some of you will even say that; "*I'm projecting this to happen*", so you can have an excuse. No, for only you control your own reality. You create what you want to be. I tested my book partially before it was published to see people's reaction to my work. Now let me ask you;

What made you, YOU?
What was your reason for choosing or reading my book?
What do you expect to get out of my book?
What would you like to see happen in your life?
What is your focus on?

Think, and think hard, for what you create deep in your subconsciousness, is a fact. This is only on "*What*", now you add the "*Why, When, Where, Who*" and the "*How's*".

Be very clear about the details of what you truly want, not what you do not want. Do you follow this …really?

People shall tell you "*this is bullshit*" except that it has been a belief that has been around for hundreds of thousands of years and it is still in practice even today. People like Anthony "Tony" Robbins,[207]

207 An American self—help author and motivational speaker. Robbins' books include "Unlimited Power: The New Science of Personal Achievement" and "Awaken the Giant Within."

Bill Gates,[208] and Shawn Corey Carter[209] are only a few among the Elite who know of this. They are not where they are because they got lucky. Modern society wants to keep you blindly unaware of this Ancient Spiritual Law.

Stay away from listening to the radio, reading the newspaper, or watching the television.

Why?

It has been proven that just watching a "*Boxing*" match means that violence is sending its energy towards you. As a result, you are responding to it and this causes violent crimes around that period. You are also showing that you are much more interested in other people's life than your own. In addition, you are consciously blocking yourself from creating your life.

Now, of course, you will come up with, what is to you along with those who think like you, is a logical excuse.

It will be "*I need to keep up with what is going on around the world*". My answer is "*keep on coming up with more excuses*" because people will always be around and will be keeping you up to date. Calculate the time you have wasted instead of doing something more productive and you will finally understand it.

Ernst (Miami) Appolon has asked me to "*explain the reasons for the use of media by the Elites and how they implement it. The reason is for its Creation and the initial test that warrants its use. How governments, companies, society and the Elites use it and all co—exist without stepping on each others toes.*

208 William Henry "Bill" Gates III is an American business magnate, philanthropist, and chairperson of Microsoft, the software company he founded with Paul Allen.
209 Better known by his stage name "Jay—Z," is an American rapper and businessperson.

How can it be used for good?
What causes the negative effects?
Why is this weapon so strong?"

All the answers to those questions shall be scattered throughout my book, however the full Truth will be hidden in "*Secret Codes*".[210]

Being successful is about enjoying life, having fun, and not being stressed. I would highly emphasis "*stress*". Now repeat after me in a super loud voice, with your teeth locked on top of each other, and speak with your lips as well as your hands in a tight fist, feel your veins popping out while you are shouting:

I AM GREATNESS AMONG GREATNESS! (pause silently in your mind) **FOR I AM POWER** (pause) **INCARNATED,** (pause) **FEARED,** (pause) **BLESSED** (pause) **AND RESPECTED** (pause) **BY ALL!**

Yes you are greatness among greatness as a consequence let no one take that away from you, not your worst enemy, not those you assume are close to you, especially, not ...**YOURSELF**!

Now bow down and ask for thanks, for the Almighty grants you your desires.

If you do not express gratitude on a daily basis, you simply will not experience all the richness you desire. The more you are grateful for, the more you shall receive as a reward.

Now relax once more, you will be alive and well. Take a deep breath in, hold it. Then exhale it. Do it a few times.

210 Refer to "Book II: Time is An Illusion" and Book III: Illuminatis The Ones and The Shadows.

Do not worry, I guarantee you will be okay when you believe.

What is holding you back from going forward?
How did you get stuck?
What is keeping you stuck?
How long has it been this way?
How long will this continue?
Who will you ask to help you?
How did this originally occur?
Did someone or an event make you stuck?

Now if you have the answers, act on them. Stop procrastinating and move forward.

What is it emotionally, mentally, and physically costing you?
What in your life is it costing the most?
How long will you tolerate this?
How much damage are you doing to yourself?

Most of you have fear in your mind; your mindset is set in doubt, worry and fear.

Your fear is about a future that has not even happened, a self—fulfilling prophecy, so stop projecting.

It all has to do with self—esteem, self—confidence, self—respect, and awareness.

Your self—esteem is ingrained in your subconscious. Therefore, if your self—esteem is low, it will always affect your self—confidence and your self—respect and will make you into who you are not. Work on all three, be in balance, do not sacrifice your life. They can only harm you if you let them harm you, do you follow?

If you think and believe you are fat or stupid, everyone will think that you are fat or stupid.

If you tell yourself; "*I have low self—esteem*", your brain registers it as a result it believes, for it does not judge.[211] Therefore, if you tell yourself, "*I have a high self—esteem*", your brain and heart will believe it. Do you follow?

Train your mind, practice until it becomes a natural habit. You pretend until you become, in your reality, what you pretend to be. Therefore, if you think positively, that is progress, for you will drown more negatives. You repel negativity and attract good things to you.[212]

You ought to get help because it becomes hard and tough. Therefore, you must build a new habit and take over your old negative manner of thinking. The Universe takes orders from your subconscious, so your subconscious belief is crucial.

Not being aware when you are in a comfortable zone is dangerous. It is not always good since you are not moving forward. What I am going over with you is in relation to the negative comfort zone where most of you are at this moment. You're mostly focusing on your personal, selfish desires and not on those who are around you, like your love ones.

I want to help you live in abundance, happy, financially free, and I want you to stay there. You may believe you have finished your path, however, in reality, you have not even started. You can hold back and let the future happen, or you can go forward and make your future.

---

211 It does not reason why.

212 Refer to Jake Hollow's "The Jake Hollow Guide on How to Persuade Women": Social Engagements Chapter 3: Negative Aspects, Chapter 4: With Women and Jake Hollow's "How to Deal with Emotions and the Life of a Motivational Speaker" Part II: Defining Emotions Chapter 1: Words Can Lie, the Body cannot.

DO YOU QUIT?

The life that you are now living;

Was it an accident?

YOU create what your life is and will be; you all have a calling with a task, you are responsible for your life. You manifest what your life is by being aware.

Most of you are less aware of your own being, but more aware of what others want to be. It's in how you think for yourself, or;

Do you let others think for you?

Many of you do not believe you have that creativity and vision in you because that is what others made you believe.

I have learned to say; "*I HAVE*" over "*I WANT*", for I am conditioning my mind and heart to believe; "*I have*", before it actually manifest its desires.

I am bringing a positive energy towards me. "*I want*", only delays. Be grateful with a positive attitude in benefit.

What has happened in your life has a lot to do with how you think. The more you think negatively about your life, the more negative things will happen to you. You created this without even realizing it. Therefore, by doing the opposite in first training your mind, you can create a vision that that you are fully conscious about. Positive or neutral[213] thinking is real. It is the way, not testing it to see if it is real, because you are bringing doubt into it.

The Universe responds to you in what you create. Ask yourself;

213 Neutral = Balance = Equilibrium.

What am I creating?

From now on, teach yourself to say only what you want and drop from your mind what you do not want. Drop all negative "*words*" and "*thoughts*". Your words and thoughts will slowly become your actions. Do this over and over repetitively.

Chapter 16

How Do You Start?

"The day you take complete responsibility for yourself, the day you stop making any excuses, that's the day you start to the top." — O.J. Simpson

Wealth.
What does wealth mean to you?

Most will say money or a great quantity of possessions or resources. Wealth is not about monetary currencies, but about all the gifts you receive when you are grateful. You can have wealth in health and a loving family, Spiritually, and even further.

When you are grateful, you will receive the same energy you are giving to the Universe. The "*Law of Gratitude*" and the Universe work together, in unison.

If you are sad or angry, seeing things more brightly and being happy, will give a cheerful reflection. By transforming your emotions to gratitude for what you have, you will attract other good things towards you. In any negative situation you can definitively find a positive perspective if you look deep enough into it.

Just focus by shifting your conscious thoughts with your subconscious into a positive view, and do not let any negative situation sneak up on you.

The moment you let any kind of negative energy touch your being, it will affect and stimulate you. If you let it win by letting it take over, the further you will sink into despair. Instead just let it flow through you.

You are building a chain reaction that is a flexible series of connected links which you have the option and freedom to act on. You can choose to follow it, into a positive, neutral, or negative path. Make a change in your life by being grateful.

Every morning before you rise out of bed, smile and say: "*I'm grateful to be up this beautiful morning once again. Today is a brand new day to chase away any surprise negative challenges that may come my way. I am so grateful for being me!*" What a great way to look at life.

Be grateful, be thankful, and show gratitude for all that is around you. If you receive a bill that has to be paid, create a place to do something thankful to have received this bill. If you did not receive this bill, you would not have gotten the service you required. This way, you will build a positive resource for more gratitude. Always be thankful, and full of cheer.

Before you retire to bed, write down all that you are grateful for so that your subconscious sets you up for good things the following day.

Once you intertwine yourself with the energy of the Universe and ask it what you want, you fully accept that it is on its way towards you as it truly does exist. You must believe, with full acceptance, without any doubt whatsoever, that it's already here, now. So, say "*thank you*" now, be grateful now. Believe it's here already, just as if you made an order through the internet or a catalogue. No matter what you have to order, act on what you asked for, so that it can manifest itself from its warehouse and be in front of you while you are not looking.

Everything that has ever happened in your life, both good and bad, be grateful for.

Why?

Because it has made you who you are now. All that you've experienced made you who you are now, at this moment. You now have to choose between going backward, forward, or staying where you are.

If you want to go forward, it is extremely essential to know how to transform your thoughts into a positive, helping way towards not only you, but also towards others. Be thankful for what you have in your life right now in the moment, what you have received in the past, and what you shall receive soon.

You now have that choice to change your life by learning from yourself. So, again, just be grateful for what brought you here because of the good and bad choices you have made in the past.

Shussh now, and do not give yourself or me any excuses. Change your view; change your life until you truly feel good about yourself by raising your energy to a high, positive light by being fully grateful. Continue this way until those feelings finally become real and integrated into a part of you.

Believe fully with your mind that life is beautiful by putting yourself in a peaceful, grateful mood and not taking your breathing for granted. Act as those who have somehow survived a near death experience and now their point of view of life has changed. They have gone back to the basics; it is the small things that now matter. Because of that experience you now enjoy life more than you ever had before.

Once you feel and sense this gratitude with a natural smile, it will have an effect on others. You are sending them your positive energy because an action creates a reaction from others. If on a regular basis you mostly have good thoughts, you will pass it on to others.

It is energy you are throwing out, so be grateful for whatever you have, had, and will receive. Be grateful for everything, for everyone, for what you drank and ate. Show real gratitude for all, and it will be ingrain, deep, deep in your heart and mind. This shall change all aspects of your life.

You may say;

How can I be grateful when I have much to be angry from in my past, present, and maybe the future?

Learn to forgive whatever has happened in all those time frames. As for the future, it has not happened yet.

Many of you live around negative energy, so once you connect with your Spiritual—self, and establish yourself in your positive "like" energy with the Universe, you will achieve your objective. Like attracts like, so you must realize that you are also connected with other beings.[214]

You have to find the source without interfering with "*other*" paths.
Accept that you are all on a mission; however, do not walk in each other's ways, just work as one.

214 We are "connected", but we are not "one" as some will claim we are.

HOW DO YOU START?

Your feelings and thoughts dictate your path's information that the Universal Energy receives. So keep yourself excited and full of joy. Now write down a minimum of five things you are grateful for,

1. ______________________________

2. ______________________________

3. ______________________________

4. ______________________________

5. ______________________________

When you are in those moments of gratitude, you are on a high vibration, so what do you think the Universe sends back to you?

It will send you more good things.

The Universe feeds off you. If it feels gratitude from you, it will send you more good things. Therefore, if you are not grateful and dwell on nothing or the opposite of your desires, then that is what you will receive back.

If you cannot forgive because you are losing things at this moment that are important to you,[215] then stay focused on the five things you wrote and feel grateful for those. Stay away from negative thoughts of loss for negative can be transformed into a positive, and that loss may lead you to something even better. In the end, what you lost will be given back to you three fold.

215 The "Lost" can be anything from a "lost love ones", "betrayal" "Lost your job/career" and the list goes on.

I. Where Are You Now?

I WOULD LOVE IT IF you, readers, would, occasionally just pause for a few minutes. Relax and let each paragraph sink into you.[216] In addition, fully, and I mean fully, focus on everything that has been written. Read every single question that has been written down in this book up to now, answer them all truthfully, first to yourself and then share them with me.

You can do that through my website, social network, or if not then through another Spiritual Teacher or Life—Coach that you may feel more comfortable with.

I would urge you to not rush when you finally do answer all the questions in my book, but that you should fully reflect on the answer you give.

What defines happiness?
What does life purpose look like to you?
Will you make yourself available?
What and why can you be thankful for when reading my book?

Do you truly understand how positive energy works; if you want the Universe to clearly perceive you?

Your life energy is strong, much stronger than what you may realize; you must intertwine yourself with the Universe's energy beyond doubt. You have to surreptitiously create[217] what you want from life.

Abraham Lincoln, once said; "*We are as happy as we make up our minds to be*". Being happy is up to each one of you. If you have a passion

216 I explain how important this is at the end of the "Introduction", if you skipped it, please go back and read the last few paragraphs in the "Introduction."
217 Done, made, or acquired by stealth.

to solve problems, like being a Spiritual Teacher or a Life— Coach, then you have that knowledge to do so.

Personally, I am overwhelmed with these gifts I have inherited and work hard to not let my ego confuse me.

Now would I be naturally searched for as a leader?

All success is based on planning, so think before you act. The best moment is when you relax and are not rushed to plan. A Life—Coach can help you realize your dreams, step by step.

You have to feel good about yourself; your self—esteem, and self—confidence, by being on top of your game.

The main way to build your self—worth is by talking in front of people as if you were motivating others on a stage as a Life—Coach.[218]

Be and act the best, be patient and a good listener.

You can achieve whatever you want if that is what you truly want. When you are not biased towards doubt, because you will be, you will find a loophole and make doubt happen. Doubt whatever should not exist in your mind, heart, or being.

I love my life, I am very happy, and feel truly fulfilled; most do not feel this way. So if you are one who does not, then I am asking you to take one hour to feel this way and say; "*I'm living the moment in a happy home*".

If you're always broke and dare to justify it with excuses that you believe are real, then you are only fooling yourself.

218 See the few last paragraphs in the "Introduction".

If you stick to your excuses instead of finding a solution, then close this book, and pass it to someone who is serious about not having excuses running their life. A step to this obstacle you call being broke is to save a minimum of ten percent of your money, by just pretending it never existed.

How can you manifest this way of thinking in your actions and attitude?

You must build your self—esteem and self—confidence. You have to accept that you are always learning, growing, and do not worry about what others think of you. When you worry about what others think of you, then your self—worth, esteem, and confidence is low.

You have control of your life. Repeat after me; "*I have control of my life and I'm very optimistic about my life. I have the drive and energy to create the life I truly deserve and want, not the life I don't want.*"

So what is holding you back in achieving this?

Even better;

What is holding you from going forward?

Training your mind is your biggest happiness.

Never give up on yourself, persist on searching for the new you.

Why?

Because the old you gets too comfortable with your old thinking pattern, while the new you is refreshed in all new aspects of positive thinking and possibilities.

So, every year bring a new you into your life. Alternatively, on your birthday, celebrate not your age, but an event, in praise of the new you that you are thankful and grateful for.[219]

You make the best of your life by being and staying successful. Every once in a while just relax, and bring out a new unpredictable you. A new refreshed you with more love for life in speed and time, financially free, and with peace of mind.

Do you control life or does life control you?

My philosophy in life is that I control my events, and get what I truly want in life.

What do you want out of your life?
What do you want in life?
Is life to work only so that you can pay your bills?

Seriously, ask yourself these questions.

You may not realize that you are getting exactly what you want, from what your subconscious creates (which is the opposite of what you want). Pause for a moment and truly think about it.

Therefore, do you agree or disagree that it is essential that you focus your energy on what you truly desire.

Why are you focused on what you do not want?

Saying, "*I don't want a crappy car/job*", shows you are focused on what you do not want. Do you follow me so far?

219 Refer to Chapter 8: The Vision Board, subtitles "I The One and Only"

While saying, "*My car/job is amazing* ... (you add the rest)" shows the opposite. It is best to focus on what you want, the positive of what you are doing and thinking. Positive energy does not just happen; you have to work on it until you peak its performance. Comprehend fully that for you, you are a Creator in your life.

You create and manifest into your life what you truly and deeply want.

Remember to believe in your psyche with gratitude.

A negative is not always wrong. Although it may appear to be negative, it is all in how you perceive it, use it, and control it.[220] For example: imagine being imprisoned for a crime you did not commit. You spend a few years in prison, and now;

Do you spend your time being depressed, vile, and violated or alive and productive?

Being optimistic in this situation may open your eyes in a positive way of life. This may not only save your life and your loved ones, but also other inmates you met in that procedure. You will now have a positive impact on more people; do you catch where I am going with this?

So, negative events are just another energy that you can turn into a positive situation.

Sometimes it takes negative energies to lead you to a positive road, so once you fully understand there are those energies, you will be able to mold them to your advantage.

220 Imagine an invisible wall falling in front of you and blocking you so that you get back on track, yet you have the choice to accept it by changing direction that will enlighten you or refuse it by smashing through it because of your ego.

This is powerful. You will create what you want with Ultimate Wisdom, Ultimate Knowledge, and Ultimate Power.

Each of you has your own philosophies in life and a way to understand them, you can upgrade your own philosophy in life to what you believe and want. I, however, do not use philosophy but a KnoWing that only I know of and it is one I do not have to justify. It is important that you seek what you truly want. If you have everything or almost everything you want, then your philosophy is working. However, if you do not have it all, then maybe your philosophy is not working.

What kinds of lifestyle are you encouraging on yourself or those loved ones?

Sometimes when I am in a dream/trance state, I receive certain visions of events that have happened, that are happening now, and that will happen soon.

When you are aware that you create the life you have been living, you will awake your thoughts to a life you truly deserve.

When you are focused on your thoughts, then good things pop—up. Compare this to thinking outside the box.

In life, I know and feel there are unlimited possibilities, that everything bad in your life is in reality a chance for you to go within yourself to make a better life.

You become what your thoughts envision. Therefore, you create what your life will be. You are each, your own Creator, and no one can create for you what you want or do not want. That is unless you give up your power to them. Do you comprehend this?

A sound business sense should be your guide when making key decisions, not emotions.

When you picked up this book, did you believe you just picked it up, or do you see that you were meant to pick it up to read it, as you secretly wished it to be there for you?

Everything happens for a reason, it is definitely not blind coincidence, but a divine plan, a Divine Provence.[221] I am empowered to provide and empowered with happiness. One problem about foreseeing the future is that once you do see it …it changes.

221 Everything happens for a reason.

Chapter 17

Obligation

"If you ever want to get the facts straight about me or the Batman, please write to the original source, myself, for the truth, instead of second guessing." — **Bob Kane**

I'm not a specific Spiritual Teacher, nor am I a Guru. I'm an in your face person. In contrast to most, I love to be questioned. That is the reason why I ask you to do some research on what I am asked to bring to you.

When your worst fears happen to you, see it as something positive. You will be surprised at how your positive energy creates a situation that will put you back on your feet.

Some will say it's "luck," while I know it is not so. To believe in luck is like giving away your power. I believe in what the wise man believes in.[222]

Re—think and say; "*This is a good time to re—think my step by following my true path of happiness*". My point is: *one door may have closed, yet a new door shall appear for you to open.*

222 Cause and Effect.

When you make your wishes heard, detach yourself from the things you expect and just let them happen. The Universe will let you know when and where you shall receive.

I shall mention it again; you are here to celebrate a wonderful life. Do not just create your life; create a magnificent life that you conceive and desire. It is you that created this moment. You manifest what you create.

Channel your positive energy to manifest the physical you; use your thoughts with positive feelings also.

Your mind is not enough; you must have your feelings involved from your whole being. Truly feel it, do not pretend it. You may have originally pretended, however, do not do that now; do not because it must come from within. Positive energy does not just happen, nor does negative energy; you make them happen.

You must be attentive inside and outside, in both your private and professional lives. Do not be a fake.

Never do anything out of obligation, since you will hold resentment. Focus on what I just wrote. Do it because you "want" to, not because you feel you have too; not because you were asked too, and surely not because you feel trapped.

You do have a choice even if you forgot you had. Your loyalty should only be to what you would want in return, as in positive energy.

I. Self—Taught

By meditating and praying, putting yourself into a trance state of mind, it will help you commune more deeply. It will also help you to have a secular mind and readily[223] achieve your worldly objectives.

It is essential in this practice, to distinguish between understanding and experiencing. Never think that what you comprehend from what was written, through my hands, has your own specific interpretation. Never speculate that what you perceive from words has become your own experience.

Learning is borrowed from others; however wisdom is gained only from direct experience. Remember that practice is a way to educate yourself with Spiritual experiences. Clarity is sharing with others; it is to know the Spirit directly.

Ego—nullification[224] carries you to a greater height.

A need to fit in shows a lack of self—confidence, self—esteem, and self—image. Do not fall into this trap. The only approval you should maintain is yours, not those from your friends, your parents, or others.

You can begin to feel good about yourself and your contributions no matter how small or big they are. You have to fully love yourself for others to love you.

I love myself; as a result, I'm not concern about who loves me. That is why people love me, and why I love them the same way I love you. To make this simple, I do not let outsiders' influences control

223 Without much difficulty.
224 When you become selfless.

my environment; *I control my own environment. Hopefully you do not misquote me on this.*

As I've written before, when you worry, you are creating a negative possibility of a future that may or may not happen. Do you truly follow my point?

Re—program yourself. You retain the right to change only when you are ready and you know exactly what you will do. You do it for yourself only. Now ask yourself;

What is it that I really want?

Once you have the answer, you can start creating that reality in your life. Before you receive it, be aware of how it will feel having the reality you want in your life. Eliminate any negative thoughts that may creep in, even negative words.

By doing good things for yourself, you will be able to do good things for others. It is essential that you write down all you want on paper,[225] for the present. Write down the life and new behaviour you want. Learn to focus and feel the new vibration of all the new seeds you planted in your subconscious mind.

The stronger you start feeling this, the more you will nurture your subconscious plants to grow. Everyday be thankful and grateful for your day. Never stop being totally grateful for living, for even a moment.[226]

When you ask the Universe, you will receive; however, it knows what time is best for you. It will not come one second before so do not

225 With a pencil and not a pen.
226 Refer to Chapter 14: Master Your Belief.

give up, it has not forgotten you. When the time is right, it will show up and you will be amazed by its brilliant timing.

Every time you re—read these books[227] that were written through my hand, just relax and let each word in every paragraph sink into you.

In your hands, you hold the Power over which life you choose. It is an awesome responsibility that most do not see nor want to see.

Your hands are very capable, yet they must be used for the right things. They must be used to reap rewards that you are capable of attaining, one—step at a time. Never stop climbing those steps.

II. How to Recognize

I WOULD EMPHASIZE THAT THE shortcut to anything you want in your life is to "*be*" and "*feel*" happy **NOW**! This has to do with intertwining and aligning yourself with the Universe following the "*Universal Law of Creation*". If you think only about things that make you happy, happy things will be drawn towards you. This sounds easy enough, however you must work on it.

The secret is kept from others as something beyond general understanding. It has to do with the "*Law of the Spirit of Life*" that sets us free from the "*Law of Sin and Death*", not with the "*Universal Law of Creation*".

Being concerned with happiness now is indeed foolishness. You do not recognize the Power of a Higher Source; it appears to you as weakness.

227 The Universal Law of Creation Chronicles.

You have been created with a desire to know what is secret, by wisdom. Certain things have been hidden for a while. Yet, now part[228] of it is known. The secret has nothing to do with having happy thoughts in order to obtain happy things; it has to do with having the mind to see clearly.

I emphasize the importance of happiness and urge you to strive to eradicate all traces of depression and sadness. When you are depressed or sad, your energy is drained, you become weak. It is possible that your negative energy inclination will overpower you. When you are happy and full of positive energy, you can overcome this negative inclination.

Are these concepts merely theories, or can you actually apply them to your life?

How can you come to terms with all the unpleasant things that happen, particularly if they are very painful and hurtful?

How can I say that everything that happens, even these painful things, is good?

I firmly believe that everything that happens, or has happened, is positive in nature. Even when confronted with adversity, I saw, for a very short period, that my belief was well founded.

Even the destructive circumstances in which I found myself[229] led to a positive outcome.[230] Therefore, I can be assured that it will eventually lead to a beneficial outcome.

---

228 Refer to Book II: Time is and Illusion and Book III: Illuminatis The Ones and The Shadows.

229 Being incarcerated and losing the love of my life.

230 I've become a calmer person, and the love I have towards my children is gentler. We have become closer.

In other words, the situation itself may be painful or unpleasant; with the exception that it will lead to a positive outcome. If you knew the positive results from the beginning, you would most likely decide that it was worth enduring this negative experience for the sake of the positive and balanced outcome. In fact;

Would it then be a negative experience at all?

Everything is seen from our own perspective.

All is possible as long as you have passion, with those dreams within you. If you can find others like you with positive energy, work as a team. It will have a ripple effect all around you. Action matters while inaction does not give results. Take this gift, one—step at a time, as this is important.

Now, even when you do not have foreknowledge, you should have faith, without any doubt whatsoever, that everything happens for a reason. Let nature take its course.

I know and believe that even the painful and negative experiences will eventually lead to something positive. From a negative experience, good emerges. In the end, it is positive to bear the negative experiences that preceded.

I believe, and know, that all situations are brought about by a Supreme Divine Providence. These are not only situations that looked embarrassing or awkward as these may eventually lead to a positive outcome. Assume that it was itself a positive event; this is also for the good. Although at the time nobody realizes that it is positive, have faith in this.

Why can you not be happy in all situations?

To put it bluntly, you are ignorant and unaware.[231] You have not developed yourself, and moreover, not even the most developed person can have the same understanding. Therefore, you cannot always see or understand that a situation is good.

Ask the purpose to understand. Ask yourself;

What is the purpose?

Let the answer come from inside, and feel this true freedom by putting value in the lifestyle and the things you want. When you can do this with confidence, you can attract anything.

This difficulty, however, is merely a product of your limited understanding, in truth, everything is good.

You control everything; you should never see yourself as victim of circumstance. All that happens to you is ordained for a purpose, one that is ultimately for your own good.

There are two kinds of good: goodness that is openly apparent, and goodness that is disguised and requires a frame of mind to appreciate it.

You each encounter situations that are upsetting, and yet, shortly afterward you see that things work out for the best.

How many times has it happened to you that you missed an arrangement to be somewhere, but because you did, you were free to use your time differently and discovered a better positive opportunity?

This inner freedom makes you one with yourself.

231 You may take this as being rude, but this is not the intention.

As I have mentioned before, wishing me good luck does not entice me because it diminishes my ability to achieve success on my own. By relying on luck, I am handing my power over to an outsider.

If you expect things to manifest, or just appear because of your belief, your will, visualization or positive affirmation, you are wrong.

You cannot make them come into existence before you "*create a flow*". This opens a path so that the energy of what you asked for can flow towards you when you are not looking.

The point to this fictional story is that you must personally get physically involved, work, and see the opportunity that is in front of you without looking too hard or you will miss out. See the signs that are in front of you that lead you on your path. You must "*create that flow*" into existence. Remember this is applied to all aspects of life as in the search for the person you will spend your life with, the career you want, the city or country that you want to live in and the list goes on.

CHAPTER 18

Take Your Time

"The creative act lasts but a brief moment, a lightning instant of give—and—take, just long enough for you to level the camera and to trap the fleeting prey in your little box." — Henri Cartier—Bresson

In order to effectively change your path to receive your wishes from the energy of the Universe, your mind must not just be in alignment with the Universe, Multiverses, Multidimensions, the Supreme Force, and your will but intertwined as one. Then you can use change as a catalyst to free up these energies for the wishes you want and demand. However, if you truly believe you are limited, then you are limited. I truly hope you follow this?

All negative influences will, and shall be, transformed into positive good. If you should question the effectiveness of this entire proposal, put it to the test and you will see its effectiveness.

By taking your time and reading this book **"OUT LOUD"**, you are connecting yourself closer to what you are reading. Writing on a sheet of paper, with the full intention to learn, will make your transformation even faster.

You may not fully grasp, understand, or comprehend what those like me[232] are working to teach you or the True meaning behind these lessons I've received. You remain partly in the dark. Remember, whatever you do, do not, and I seriously mean this, do not assume you follow or understand what has been written through my hand until you 'decipher' the hidden 'codes' through your Spiritual Self and not from your physical ego self. [233]

The way you feel indicates if you are following negative or positive flows. It is your choice to simply push it away.

How do you perceive this when it is negative energy that is in your path?

Instead of always focusing on how to put your thoughts and words on a positive wave, make your emotions and feelings also a part of the action. That way you can raise your energy and vibrate alongside with the Universe in tune as one.

Feel and think good, then you will naturally stay empowered with your thoughts. This will make you feel good inside so this will show on the outside, automatically drawing all your dreams and wishes towards you.

The flow of good things will come easier for you. This I can promise you.

It is extremely important for you to love, honour, and respect yourself since the Universal Consciousness feels and senses your True Being and will only look after you if you look after yourself.

232 Receiving from a Higher—Source

233 Refer to "Book II: Time is An Illusion" and Book III: Illuminatis The Ones and The Shadows.

So, when you think that you are not worth much, you are sending out the message that you are not important to the Universe.

The Universal Consciousness will send back to you exactly what you sent it ... that you are not worth much and that is what you will attract back. Otherwise, the better you feel about yourself, the higher your vibrational energy will be. The Universe will receive that frequency.

Is that not what you want?

Show the Universe that you value yourself and that you will find more good things that flow towards you. Become alive, become full of joy and design your future now by creating what is "rightly yours". Know that anything is possible, for you are the Creator of you, and your happiness will attract others, like you, into your life.

I. The Closer You Become

WORDS ONLY MEAN SOMETHING WHEN something is attached to them. If you lived the life you wanted, you would most likely truly be happy; however, this does not mean life would be perfect. It can merely lead you to peace of mind.

The Universe always finds ways to leave you signs. On the radio, newspaper, television, in ancient relics, in art, or just a word and some images you see that release a memory trigger mechanism. The Universe lets you see the signs at the right moment it chooses. For instance, a movie, a book, or a visual website you visited a few times, yet you never noticed or saw any signs until just that moment.[234] Do you follow what I mean by this? This is very important to understand.

234 The sign was not there, until that exact moment it should. Not before or after.

Now why is it that you did not notice or sense it before?

It is for the reason that your awareness was not awaken at that moment or the time just was not right.

You must find others who have these special gifts to share the knowledge you have, so that you can combine them together into its real meaning.

Those who have eyes that see what your Spiritual Self sees, find ways to help those who desire it.

Do not judge any information you may receive wherever you may have received it, just listen and take notes. Use your visualization ability to clear the energy. Clear any dark or clogged energy breathing, and your energy will open an energy path.

Visualize and clearly see your positive energy moving gently with it in connection with the Universal Life Force. At this moment, you are fully connected and you are beyond the Universal Law of Creation.

It is one thing to be able to read words and sentences and another is to comprehend what you have read. It is quite another to then take what you read, pretend comprehension, and apply it in a real physical sense of your life.

Under the law of "*like attracts like*", a magnetic energy field, the reflection of the inner person, will attract to it compatible energy fields.

Everything is energy. Energy is consciousness, consciousness is energy. They are the same. Your energy field becomes infused with its energy.

Those close to me will reunite with who I became, some as my friends, some as foes to a friend, and once more into a bride. It is time for the Power Within.[235]

II. Undesirable Matters

Most people are stressed because they are not rooted, not truly connected to the Universe.

I personally pull up my life force energy as one with the Universe, Multiverses, Multidimensions, and Spiritual Realm, while Roman Brave simply connects himself from the Earth outward.

He imagines himself as a tree where his feet are rooted deep into the Earth, just as a strong tree (the Teak Tree or Tectona Tree).[236] Then he pulls up the Earths energy from the roots and draws it into his body to feel energized.

Others use the Air or Water elements; I ground myself directly with all the Universes, Multiverses, and Multidimensions.

There is no wrong or right. On the contrary, it is the level you are at. It does not matter how you do it as long as you achieve that feeling of deep Spiritual connection.[237]

The subject of Dark Force, and Spiritual Entities, is not a very popular one.

235 Reality changes by taking another path which can be followed in Book II: Time is an Illusion.

236 Is one of the tropical hardwood birches. This tree is originally from the plantations of South East Asia, and can grow to a height of thirty to forty meters.

237 Refer to Chapter 14: Master Your Belief.

The idea that something and "*not you*"[238] is somehow influencing[239] your actions or affecting your life is not a fun thought. It is maybe even a little bit scary.

Here is good news: Nothing or no one can harm you without your permission, even if that permission is on an emotional or soul level rather than a conscious one. Learn to separate your "*Soul—Self*" from your "*Spiritual—Self*" since they are not the same. One is who you are now physically, the other is infinity.

When compared to the physical level, carrying around Spiritual Entities is like having parasites. They are parasites, but what you regard as dark force is on the Spiritual Plane.

I have what you will call a theory about entity possession, however, in my reality, it is a fact and the Truth; what you call an entity, bad spirit, or even a demon or Jinn's, can safely be termed as negative energy. "*Bad energy*" are some things are "*nourished*" with negative emotions, like anger and fear.

If you have physical parasites, you would want to make your body inhospitable to them; you use herbs or homeopathy the bugs do not like; maybe even stop eating what they like you to eat.

With spiritual parasites, the approach is sometimes similar to something to run the bugger off, and to make yourself a "bad host." This will usually mean a change in attitude or behaviour, sometimes even a change of environment.

238 Physical You.
239 Your Higher—Self, Your True Spiritual—Self.

Purifying your thoughts is not always so easy. This may be why people[240] came up with the idea of group worship services.[241] It is a lot easier to maintain a positive persona in a group of like—minded people.

So, be careful with who you are with. You never know "*who else*" might be there, too, just waiting to hitch a ride.

When you find yourself in the midst of a crisis, it may not have to do with the event, but more about how much you let it affect you. Yes, it is true that it is hard to control thoughts; however, you have the ability to focus your thoughts with the help of your heart.

A negative thought demands too much attention. Which of the following three ways would you choose to relate to me:

Accept and to continue to think about the subject, even though you know they are undesirable.

Block them and force it out.

Simply ignore it and focus on another matter, and let it flow out on its own.

The third would be your best and logical answer.

Why?

Be your own teacher and figure it out, and then email me your answer.

240 Being human.
241 Church, temple, and circle.

Most of you enjoy subconsciously focusing on negativity because you are not ready to go out and face life.

You would rather wallow in despair instead of going out and break through any barriers that stand in your way.

Intense thoughts about other persons have often produced very positive effects. Think positively, and the outcome will be good.

Put yourself in a state of mind that radiates confidence that shows that you believe it shall happen, and then it will. When you are in a High Spirit, your function improves with positive thinking. It brings positive change.

By envisioning good in your mind, you create positive Spiritual influences that enable that picture to materialize.

This is the "*Universal Law of Creation*": you attract what you want. You will attract all the joy and peace you require. By having this confidence and inner strength to face challenges, you generate a positive divine influence.

When you trust and rely on the "*Universal Law of Creation*", you attract what you want and you create a situation that will allow you to use your energy in a positive and beneficial way. Your positive thoughts serve as catalysts that promote favourable circumstances.

III. Get Involved

You are what you think and you create your own reality. Effective manifestation happens when you are fully using the energy with all your being.

Energy of this material "*thing*" has power, not the "*thing*" itself. Once you see this illusion is not being the "*thing*", you will let it go.

If you do not get out of that rut, you will continue creating polarity between your mind, body, and Spirit. Go to the root of the issue and issue a change level.

Whatever you believe in certainly has power, since whatever is fuelled by energy has power. My point here is about energy of creation, it applies to manifestations.

Therefore, if you stop making excuses and give yourself the Power to Create something out of nothing, there is Power here.

The object of your Creation does not necessarily have Power; the act of doing begins to change things. You have opened your creative centers by doing.

By being willing to do something with nothing, you have taken your Power back. You have aligned your will. You have created something.

This is what has the ability to propel you forever. This is called transformation. You are taking a negative and making it into a positive.

Form follows thought; thoughts have real energy. What you say and think becomes an integrated belief system; it therefore becomes true.

If you are convinced, you are limited because you do not have enough. You have now limited yourself and your funds. If you believe that there are no limitations, then it will be unlimited.

You require setting an intention with your mind and most importantly, you must be willing to take responsibility for what you create.

This begins to intertwine the will of the ego with the "*Universal Will*". Taking responsibility helps you remove fear that blocks the Energy of Creation. Not responding to what you created renders you powerless.

Get proactive and learn. Figure out what you can do and then do it. Doing this will help you remove the fear you have learned as a consequence of others belief systems. Most of you do not see that what you have asked to manifest is in front of you. As a result, you "*turned it down*", lost faith, and wondered why the Universe did not save you.

It was in front of you, however, you did not notice it. You missed one of your opportunities.

IV. Principle

Learn to instruct yourself by having no regrets. Stop blaming people or circumstances, for this will not move you forward, it will keep you stuck. You always have a choice even if you do not like the choice; you have the option to open yourself in infinite possibilities.

If you do not open yourself, you limit the Universe's ability to work in your life. Limited thinking produces limited results.

Ask for your desires to manifest, just do not worry about the "*how*". You cannot manifest anything while you are working hard to control the "*how, when*" and "*where*".

Just know that you shall get it. Nothing can happen when you insist on being in control of the situation.

Let go, relax, and let it happen, so that the pathway is open for the Universe to work its miracles and bring you what you desire.

If it is a relationship you want, you must let go and set it free so that you can give it the opportunity to transform. Once you do let go completely, do not be attached to the outcome, don't chase it, control where it goes, or give it instructions.

When you feel ungrateful for something, you make yourself a victim, thus rendering yourself powerless to create and manifest during the time you remain in that mind frame.

Start with being grateful for having a means to open the pathway towards good things, whether you feel like this or not. What stands in the way of being grateful is the distortions of your illusion versus your desire.[242]

Being fully grateful, even briefly, has the effect of moving you out of your negative patterns, illusions, or belief systems. As a result it opens a pathway for abundance of all sorts you can return to easily and effortlessly.

I wrote down that you should teach yourself. Blame takes away your power. Blaming others or yourself dis—empowers[243] you, however

242 Refer to Chapter 16: How Do You Start?
243 To deprive of power, authority, or influence: make weak, ineffectual, or unimportant.

taking responsibility pulls your Power back. Forgiving and being thankful also brings and pulls Power to you. Look for the blessing in what and why this happened to you. The awareness you have can help recognizing where you are.

Appreciate what you have and help yourself first so that you can help others. In order to spread love, you must first love yourself; so study love, the principles of love, the way you personally understand it, and you shall attract love towards you.

A bright attitude shall be a barrier against all things you may want to keep out of your life. Your superb mood will attract more happy positive people towards you.

With all this, you will have a good Spirit once you are truly in tune with the Universes' frequencies. Not because you say you are, but because of your actions and those others see in you. Once you truly get this, you will make yourself immune even to your own self.

Chapter 19

What Do You Crave?

"I believe in God, but not as one thing, not as an old man in the sky. I believe that what people call God is something in all of us. I believe that what Jesus, Mohammed, Buddha, and all the rest said was right. It's just that the translations have gone wrong." — **John Lennon**

The reality you are living in is truly a physical visual illusion that your mind makes real in a world of optical illusion. You have to lose yourself along with any fears, doubts, and disbeliefs.

If you want to be distinguished, do not "*think*" you are distinguished, but "*know*" that you are distinguished. This all has to do with the Universal Secret Laws in Manifesting "*your*" Dreams.

When you see a solid object, you do not see the object; the object is only an illusion that appears real and is not really there; there is only energy that is vibrating at a certain frequency.

To a One Dimensional being, you would be seen as a g—d.

How can I explain this?

Imagine that you somehow entered a One Dimensional reality and then made an effort to communicate with the life beings there. There will be one problem. They will only see an imprint of your feet when you walk, while you can see everything.

Why?

They are one dimensional beings. Up does not exists in that reality. Do you follow?

Most of you are not even ready to be awakened. As a result, those of you who are not ready shall only see what you believe is real and what is Truly real will not exist in your view.

When you are ready, you will not have to even question the path you would require to take, you will just know it.[244]

There is a deeper meaning when you cherish material possessions over immortal souls. On a deeper level, you appreciate the physical presence more than the Spiritual identity. The first would die while the latter continues in Existence in the Immortal Soul for Eternity.

Most of you crave to remain connected to your physical bodies. After all, this is the only person you know; your immortal soul is cloaked in a mortal physical body.

However, as sad as it may be, a physical body does not live forever and your Spirit lives on. It can never be destroyed, for it is energy.

By having thoughts, you can control your Creative Power. Whatever you may form in your thoughts, hold on to it. It must come

244 Refer to "Book II: Time is An Illusion", will have a more indicative explanation on this subject.

into existence as a visible material form in the physical reality, whether or not it becomes visible to everyone else's eyes. It shall become real, it will manifest itself. So surround yourself with these invisible forms you associated in your thought, until they become solid for all to see.

By the "*Law of the Universals Creed*", if you desire something, then clearly picture it clearly, in detail, in your mind and heart. Then steadily hold onto that image until it becomes a definite thought form.

With practice, the things you want will come to you in material form when you least expect it and not a moment before or after you want it. It must do so in obedience to the Law by which the Universe was Created.

Close your ears to all actively opposed suggestions and never mind if people call you a fool. It is just a lack of judgement; just dream on for you know the Truth.

Do not be misled by false notions of duty or obligation to others. You have no possible duty or obligation to anyone that should prevent you from making the most of yourself.

Be true to yourself; just follow your instincts and you will be honest with everyone. Once you have fully decided what you want to be, then form the highest conception that you are capable of imagining and make that conception a formed thought. Hold it as a fact, as the real Truth about yourself, and believe in it.

Keep your ideals of what you wish to make of yourself and be sure that you make the right choice.

Make a thought form that you are healthy, strong, and hearty. See yourself as intelligent; practice this every moment you have. Don't violate this Ancient Law for which the physical body is built. Your thought will become real and in the flesh. This is "*certain*" for it comes by obedience to the Universal Laws.

Make yourself as you desire to be by changing your thoughts into a physical illusion you call reality. See it as your imagination is capable of forming that conception.

I. Don't Dwell On It

As Spiritual Life—Coaches, once we have shown or proven that our theories are valid and true, you will begin to follow the belief and judgment we provide.

I have noticed that the demand for Spiritual Life—Coaches has gone up while more people seek advice. However, be careful for I foresee many false Spiritual Life—Coaches in my visions.[245]

These instructions are that I've received is that you have to learn to observe, by having perfect faith in yourself. I personally no longer think with doubt or make mistakes as before. Yes my physical—self can get upset and even lose track, yet I catch myself.

"*When you prepare yourself for the worst, the best shall happen*". In other words, never look at a negative situation as a negative; it can lead you to a positive "*when*" you have total perfect faith, not "*if*" you have faith.

Once you believe all of this, you shall receive and see it happening when you least expect it. You are going through the flow instead of anticipating the outcome; you are grateful for whatever comes.

245 Refer to "Book III: Illuminatis The Ones and The Shadows", Chapter 2: Hidden Clues, subtitle "III Negative Freedom"

As long as you hold onto your thoughts and faith, all will go according to your wishes. In other words, your Spiritual Higher—Self Plans.

For as long as you do not doubt yourself, your attitude, or your power to create, then nothing can be or go wrong. Fully trust without any doubt whatsoever and do not be afraid. Banish, and I mean banish, all negative thoughts from your mind without any excuses.

Don't rush towards your desire because to hurry is a manifestation that shows fear "*You are giving away your Power to Create.*"

You are violating the "*Ancient Universal Laws*". By not having fear, you show that you have plenty of time for what you want, manifesting it with patience and trust. I will never be too early or too late since nothing shall or will go wrong.

Your vision must become your goal and your mission your commitment. You must obey the "*Universal Consciousness*" without question; it gives you the Power to Create. It must do so in obedience to the Law by which the Universe was Created.

If ever it appears to go wrong, do not feed into its trap, and do not let it disturb your mind — it is an illusion. It just appears as if it is going wrong. Nothing can go wrong in your world except for you getting the wrong mental attitude. It is all a state of mind or an allowance of feeling.

Whenever you do find yourself in these situations, where you get overly excited, worried or mentally rushed, then just relax, sit down and think. All will be right at the right moment when you least expect it to be.

If you do not follow these simple teaching,[246] you will instantly cut your connection with the Universal Mind. You shall receive no power, no knowledge, and no wisdom until you are calm. By this, the principle of power within you is caged and you turned your strengths into weakness.

Whatever you do, do not think of yourself as limited in power or as a failure. If that is what you think, that is who you are. Do you follow me on this?

You must now form a greater and better "*attitude with habit*", and form your belief as a being of limitless power. Your habits decide your destiny, so change your habits of thinking.

Thinking you are great or that you are the best, only once in a while, does not help. So increase your prayers, trancing or meditation to help you think that way. Change your habit of thought to a time when you know that you are the best and greatest there is, ever was, and ever will be.

II. Storm Wave

To be a Spiritual Teacher is not easy. In fact, we[247] are judged more strictly than others. There are those of you who will cause disorder and trouble just because you are full of bitterness, jealousy as well as selfishness. Those of you who do not want to see us succeed will lie to cover up the Truth, which will show that you have no true wisdom.

If any of my readers is lacking wisdom, then continue asking and visualize; it will be given to you generously without reproach.

246 That has been secretly around before time itself existed.
247 I personally do not consider myself a Spiritual Teacher or a Guru.

So keep on asking in total faith, picture it clearly in your mind and hold onto that thought steadily. Your heart must be beyond any shadow—of—a—doubt for if you doubt even for as little as a microsecond, it will be like a wave from the sea tossing what you have asked for around in its storm. It is that sensitive.

What you have asked for was on its way towards you, but now it is lost in the sea. Just by that small doubt. Do not expect it to arrive, for you have disrespected the Natural Universal Law of Creation. You have shown that you are an indecisive, unsteady person in all your ways to it.

It means you cannot make up your mind, so surely you cannot be trusted.

At this moment, do not expect the Universe to give you anything at all. The alignment you intertwined with it has been broken and you created a domino effect that affects all other things you asked for. You require finding that link again, or starting all over again, to intertwine yourself with the Universe.

My readers, how do you benefit if you say you believe and have faith yet you do not truly practice it?

Please, please do yourself a favour and throw this book out, destroy it, burn it or do whatever with it. Just stop reading it if you cannot apply by these Ancient Laws.

If you ask out of selfishness, you shall not receive, since you are asking with wrong expectations. You only receive from total selfless love.

Banish all negative doubts from your mind, learn to drop all doubts. Then transform them into trust and faith. If not, what is the point to continue reading what was written through my hand and cry for help if you don't practice by following the Universal Laws.

Do your own research on this, for these are not my laws.

Are you like those who stare at themselves in a mirror and then quickly forget how they look like when they walk away?

Do you have to go back to make sure that you saw correctly and that it was not an Illusion?

The Universe must follow in obedience to the Law by which it was originally created, not violating this Ancient Law, it is certain.

The prospective of reality that you allow is what you see;

So how do you break out of this illusion?

Do not accept it and, at the right moment, it shall change. You choose the suggestion you want!

You are a Spiritual being enjoying space—time. In this physical body, you may not be able to walk through a wall, yet in reality you can stop some of these limitations you created for yourself.

As a Spiritual being, you keep returning to the physical flesh because it is a fun game. Sometimes, you return more than once to the same life just to re—live it or change some events.

III. Where Do You Want To Be?

EVERYTHING THAT HAPPENS IN THIS physical reality is the result of a thought and emotion. If you change your thoughts, you change your physical reality.

Look closely at your reality as if you are looking at what you think and feel of yourself at the very core of your being.

It is easier to look outside yourself so that you can find somebody else to blame for what is happening to you. However, be truthful to yourself. You attracted these experiences. The answer lies within yourself, not outside of you.

You are absorbing energy from the Universe and the Higher Level of yourself. You are transmitting that energy all the time through[248] and into the world. As that energy passes through you, it picks up your energy pattern.

This precisely reflects your emotional, mental, physical, and Spiritual state of mind. Through these means, the subconscious creates a physical duplicate of itself which reflect its sense of self before your eyes, in people, places, and experiences.

At any moment, in any day, you are casting around yourself and creating an image of what you think of yourself. It is this that creates your reality by attracting to you experiences which corresponds to that pattern.

If you believe and think that you will always be poor, penniless and puny, that is the energy pattern you will cast around you. This

248 Like Roman Brave would say; "Chakra system"

will attract poverty and lack of confidence to you on the basis of "*like attracts like*".

However, if you Believe and think it's your Birth Right to always be mentally, emotionally, physically and Spiritually healthy and wealthy, in all aspects of life, including materially rich, and that you deserve it, these things will become your reality.

This energy pattern which you send out around yourself attracts the experiences and opportunities to manifest in your life what is going on inside.

There is going to be those around you who will claim that this belief is all but a fraud and with the same breath say; "*I am confident of achieving my dreams*", but in the end, they never do. That is because deep down they know they are the fraud and expect that others are like them. Words hide what is inside us, while actions speak louder.

Teach yourself how to de—program this feeling and thinking. You can only truly be free when you respect and love yourself. What you think and feel is what you create, and what you think is based on what you feel and know.

For a frequency that carries information and knowledge, the higher the frequency, the more developed and evolved the knowledge.

IV. Forgiveness?

For all that you have done, whether good or bad, you must recognize, accept, and forgive not only others, but yourself. You must connect yourself with the Universe; collect this positive awesome energy and win forgiveness for yourself. However, you can hardly expect to be forgiven or forgive yourself if you have not been willing to forgive others.

Forgiveness is not easy; it requires work. It is more important to connect and intertwine[249] yourself with the Universe and the Universal Law of Creation. You must be in peace with who you are. Therefore;

How can positive outcomes come to you if you have not been willing to truly forgive others?

This only attracts the opposite of positive, a negative aspect of you. Now is the ideal time to feel this positive connection, for if this was not true, you would not be reading my book.

The secret of being able to forgive others is to remember that you are reading this, and that whatever belief you may have, you "know" you were given life for an unknown reason.

You matter; you have a vital, essential and irreplaceable importance and role to play in this life. When you accept and remember this, you will have the strength to rise above the pain others have caused you and forgive both them and yourself.

Forgiving does not mean you are forgetting or accepting those who betrayed you in your past life, but only that you are a better person. It is stronger to forgive. Do not take it as a weakness.

249 Once you intertwine yourself with the Universe, forgiveness "will" become easier.

Life is meant to be a circle encompassing all your experiences and relationships in one harmonious, seamless whole. When someone hurts you, the circle is broken. Forgiveness is the way you mend the fracture. Forgiveness means not merely forgiving the person who hurt you, but forgiving yourself, forgiving whatever you believe in, like a Higher Intelligence, forgiving even life itself with all its bizarre and often cruel twists and turns. This applies even if you are an atheist.

Once you forgive, the circle is again complete and you will find yourself encompassed by the wholeness of the Universe of which you are an integral part. Then you can have the confidence to really stay strong, be at peace with yourself, and finally heal.

The moment you say "*never*", is the day it will happen.[250] You say you will "*never*" cheat or never abandon people or someone you love, but the next thing you know, you did the opposite. That is pride, and then you look for excuses to justify yourself in breaking your own promises and rules.

Learn not to think too hard about doing wrong, but "*focus*" more on your Spiritual—Self to guide you in being sensible, wise, and apologize to those you hurt. Say it with your whole heart and forgive yourself. Do not let pride and ego destroy you. You must mean it from deep inside your heart and not because you were discovered, but because you know it is right. Humility leads to real honour.

250 Without realizing it, you were focused on the negative

V. Before?

FRIENDS, BE GLAD, EVEN IF you are facing many difficulties. You must learn to endure them, so that you are completely mature and do not lack in anything.

If you require wisdom, you should just ask for it and it will be given to you. However, when you ask for something, you must believe in it fully with faith and do not doubt it. If you have any doubts with the frequency you are sending out there, it is as if an ocean wave tossed them around in a storm as was written before.[251] This shows that you cannot make up your mind, and that you cannot be trusted. So do not expect to receive anything at all.

You will receive it, only if you have pure faith, and you have not give up truly believing without any doubt whatsoever. Ask, Believe, and as a result you will receive; see your reward with a glorious life, like all those who believe.

Do not blame others when you are tempted by negative thoughts! You are tempted by your own desires that will drag you off and trap you. Your desire makes you blind. When they finish with you, it leaves you dead. Do not be fooled, my dear friends. Every good and perfect gift comes if your thoughts are pure and positive.

You should be quick to listen and slow to speak or get angry. If you are frustrated and angry, you cannot do any good. Instead, be humble and accept by calming your negative signal, transforming it into positive energy.

251 II Storm Wave.

Do not fool yourself by just asking. If you do not have faith and believe it, you are like those people who stare at a mirror and forget how they look as soon as they turn away.

You must never stop looking at the perfect law that will set you free. You will receive everything you want, if you sincerely Ask, and truly Believe. Do not just see then forget. As an example; you've made an order of an item you expect to be delivered to you, yet just before a Federal Express driver arrives to your door to deliver what you asked for, you waved him off. This would be the same.

What good is it to say you believe when you do nothing to show that you really do?

If you saw someone considered poor because they are dressed in rags with no food, would you say to this person; "I hope all goes well for you. I hope you will be warm and eat well." Or do you simply give them pocket change?

What good is it, unless you help and show them the way?[252]

So, remember your frequency must not be in contradiction to your will. If you say, "*I do not want to lose her/him*".

What are you really saying or feeling?

Your frequency misunderstood it as; "*I will lose her/him!*" it feeds off your "*fears*", since your fear is in losing her/him. That energy comes out stronger from your subconscious. Yet if you eliminate this negative fear, and totally condition your thoughts and feelings that you will not lose her/him, "*you shall not*". Make an effort by saying; "*I am in her/*

252 Give them an opportunity, not a hand out. The rest is up to them to accept or refuse.

his heart, as a result she/he is in mine. We are one, and we are stronger together!" Do you see the difference?

You absolutely must believe in it, without any shadow—of—a—doubt, or else what would be the point in just saying it, if you do not feel it or believe it.

Are you wise or sensible?

Then show it by living right and by being humble and wise in everything you do. If your heart is full of bitter jealousy and selfishness, do not brag or lie to cover up the truth. Whenever people are jealous or selfish, they cause trouble and do all sorts of cruel things.

True wisdom comes from those who are pure, friendly, gentle, sensible, kind, helpful, genuine, sincere, but will not let people take them for granted.

But, once they find this Ancient Scripture about asking for their energy and connecting themselves with the Solar System with total faith, believing without any doubt without testing this as if it is just a theory, they will receive their wish.

Never ask with selfish intent; it must come from your heart and thoughts. You must **FEEEEEL** it and **SEEEEE** it before you receive it. Purify your heart, if you cannot make up your mind. Stop laughing and start crying.

Be glad instead of gloomy. Be humble and honour yourself. My friends, do not say cruel things about others! If you do, or if you condemn others, you are condemning yourself three times over. By doing this, you are reflecting by throwing a curse on yourself.

What right do you have to condemn anyone?

Never take an oath by swearing on anything. "*Yes*" or "*No*" is all that you are required to say. If you say anything more, you will be condemning yourself.

Your belief can be Spiritual or religious. If you have "*faith*" when you "*align*" and "*intertwine yourself*" with your "*belief*", and you wish someone you know is sick to become well, then they will get well.

As long as you have no doubt, and no selfish agenda, this person will be well. It really does take many negative thoughts and persistent negative thinking to bring something negative into your life.

Ask, and believe fully in your heart and mind that you already have your desires, and know in the unseen, you will have shifted your desire into the perceived. Do you follow where I am going?

If so, then email me your perception to me and I may publish them in my next book.

However, if you persist in thinking negative thoughts over a period of time, they will appear in your life. If you worry about having negative thoughts, you will attract more, multiplying them at the same time.

If you pay close attention to your thoughts and notice that your thoughts contain "*doubts*" just because you do not have your item yet, you will continue to attract it by not having it yet. Decide right "*now*" that you are going to think only positive, good thoughts. Believe you already **HAAAVVEEE** it, **FEEEEEL** it, and do not second—guess it. Say to yourself: your positive, good thoughts are powerful while focusing that your negative bad thoughts are weak.

Do not let your life be controlled by your desires. Control your desires. You are here to learn or evaluate what you already knew, but if you are a rude person or a control freak, then stop being so hateful!

Quit attempting to fool people and start being sincere. Do not be jealous or say cruel things about others.

If you truly knew all this, then you are a teacher, and an example to others. You no longer have an excuse like those who do not know. Do not take my word on this, but do your own research and come up with your own conclusion.

I beg you to not surrender yourself to this negative thinking, but to fight it.

You see, even at my weakest moment people believed in me, and helped me, which woke my subconscious, to my True deep desire.

Do you really love life?

Do you want to be happy?

Then stop being cruel and quit telling lies. Give this up, and follow the road that will lead you to peace.

Can anyone really harm you for being eager to do good deeds?

Continue even if you have to suffer for doing good things. Stop being afraid, do not worry about what people might do. The more you think positively, the easier these people will disappear. The moment you worry, though, the more you bring the negative energy back.

Always be ready to give an answer when someone asks you about your hopes. Give a kind and respectful answer and keep your conscience clear. This way you will make them ashamed for saying bad things about your good conduct. It is better to suffer by doing right than to suffer for doing wrong.

Dear friends, do not be surprised or shocked. You are being tested as if you are walking through fire.

Be glad for the chance to suffer now. It has prepared you for even greater happiness later. Count a blessing when you suffer because now you understand and show that you are willing to move away from it. This will make you complete, steady, strong, and firm.

Stay positive, not simply because you think you must, but let it be something you want to do instead of something you do merely to make money.

Some false Spiritual Life—Coaches out there teach. They sneak in and speak harmful lies to you saying; "It is my way! You have to follow my teachings, for I've studied these subjects for years; follow my doctrine!" I say we are each unique and you should do your own research and do what is best for you.

Who am I too say my way is right?

Some people will read this book and fully understand what I am all about while some people will destroy themselves by twisting what was written. My dear friends, you have been warned ahead of time! So do not let the errors of these people pull you down the wrong path, making you lose your balance. Keep on growing.

CHAPTER 20

Other's View Points

"A human being is a part of the whole that is called universe by us, a part limited in time and space. We experience ourselves, our thoughts and feelings as something separate from the rest. A kind of optical of consciousness. This is a kind of prison for us, restricting us to our personal desires and to affection for a few persons nearest to us. Our task must be to free ourselves from the prison by widening our circle of compassion to embrace all living creatures and the whole of nature in its beauty. The true value of a human being is determined by the measure and the sense in which they have obtained liberation from the self. We shall require a substantially new manner of thinking if humanity is to survive." — **Albert Einstein**

I. Maktub

Maktub: (Arabic).

Meaning: It was "**written**".

MY NAME IS MICHAEL AND I am writing this testimonial from Donald Wyatt Correctional Facility.[253]

253 This a private—enterprise detention prison in the town of Central Falls, Rhode Island (U.S.).

While sitting in a segregation cell[254] (also known as "*The Hole*") as a consequence of my actions, I had the opportunity to read a book called "*The Alchemist*".[255] In this book, I came across the defined word "maktub", but I did not know how to pronounce it.

The Alchemist details the journey of a young Andalusian shepherd boy named Santiago. Santiago, believing a recurring dream to be prophetic, decides to travel to the pyramids of Egypt to find treasure. On the way, he encounters love, danger, opportunity, and disaster. One of the significant characters that he meets is an old king who tells him that "*When you want something, all the universe conspires in helping you to achieve it*". This is the core philosophy and motif of the book.

When I was released from segregation, I was brought to a new block. I was in search of a person who spoke Aramaic. The first person I asked was wearing a Taqiyah,[256] to which he replied with a "*no*", and pointed to a cell a couple of doors down to a person who might understand Aramaic. When I got to the door, I saw a middle aged man with long black hair kept back in a ponytail. He had a goatee and glasses and was writing in a deeply concentrated way. While watching him through the small window on his door, I did not want to disturb his concentration; however, he had already sensed I was there by his door, so I asked:

Excuse me, do you speak Arabic?

He stood up, walked towards me, stood next to me in the doorway, and looked me straight in the eyes with his reply;

254 To isolate from others.

255 The Alchemist (Portuguese: O Alquimista) is an allegorical novel by Paulo Coelho first published in 1988. It has been hailed as a modern classic. The Alchemist was originally written in Portuguese and has since been translated into 67 languages, winning the Guinness World Record for most translated book by a living author. It has sold more than 65 million copies in more than 150 countries, becoming one of the best—selling books in history.

256 Also spelled "Tagiyah," is a short, rounded cap worn by Muslim men

No, I do not, but why do you ask?

At that moment, I told him about the word I had come across and the meaning given. I told him I was seeking someone who spoke Arabic, for the correct pronunciation.

After a few minutes of conversation, I realized we had a lot of the same interests in common. Moreover, after more in—depth and personal conversations, I found out our fathers died on the same calendar day. Now there is a long story behind the date of my fathers' death. Before my father died, this number had been a sign that had been leading me to many things over the past three years. As a result, it led to my father's death or, he happened to die on the same day, as that particular number. Now I realize that I was supposed to meet this man, because of the number. Also our fathers died on the same day. I know this not only because of the number, but also because of how we met. The word Maktub. "*Because it was written.*"

I had the honor of reading his rough draft of a book he was finishing. Following this, I saw the reason why we were supposed to meet, and it was clear. We have the same Spiritual belief.

Let me tell you a little about this man's work. His name is Lord Master Archangel DiCaprio. Here is an example:

We hear horror stories of murders. Mothers killing babies; husbands killing wives, and then themselves. In contrast, we think to ourselves, "*How could a person have so much negativity within themselves to commit such a terrible thing?*" These people are seen as evil, but they were not always like that. Try to visualize that person as a five year old child, laughing, smiling, and just being a child. Think about how innocent that child was, filled with pure positive energy before this negative energy affected that Child's world. Every one of us can recall at least one time in our childhood lives when we were completely happy and stress—free.

Lord DiCaprio's teachings and techniques provide you with the essential knowledge to rebuild your self—esteem and confidence. It gets you back to the positive energy you once possessed that provided you with internal happiness. Lord DiCaprio's book gives you simple steps that you can do now, as you are reading and bettering yourself. Whether it is picking up women or just becoming one with who you are Spiritually. As a result, the sooner you put these steps into action, the sooner you will be back to the happy and confident person that has been missing for so long.

With an awareness to identify the positive and negative energy that you subconsciously create, control them before the negative overpowers the positive energy. Not only will you become aware and be able to identify them, you will become selective to the energies you allow into your Spiritual Realm. You will become more selective of the people you communicate with, do business with, as well as spend your quality time with, following this way. You will have surrounded yourself with only positive people.

Positive energy creates positive energy while negative energy creates negatives energy. By doing this, not only will you become happier, confident, as well as stress free. Also, you will grow as a community of Spiritual Beings. So you are not changing yourself, you are changing the world.

In the "*Secrets and Laws of the Universe*", he explains that what you put out to the Universe, you get back. So if you put negative, you get negative back. As with positive, you get positive back. That is the Law of the Universe.

OTHER'S VIEW POINTS

I tested Lord DiCaprio teachings. Once I was one in my Spiritual Realm trancing, I told the Universe "*my lawyers and I are communicating, we're resolving an issue that has been put off for a long time*", but in the physical reality, we had not been in contact or even communicated in a while. One of my lawyers that I had not heard from in three years, however on the other hand I am in a place where I am unreachable by the outside world.[257] I did this trancing state of art everyday for a little over two weeks.

In the meantime, I had left the power of attorney to my mother. When I saw my mother she told me; "*Michael, you will not believe it, as it's the strangest thing. Both of your lawyers called for you in the same week, and both have great news for you.*" One of those lawyers went a step further to search for me and found me. Therefore, this was the proof that was needed. When I told Lord DiCaprio about what had happened, he gave me that confident, humble smile.

Over the past couple of months, living in the same block with Lord DiCaprio, we have had the opportunity to brainstorm on a daily basis. He has helped me become one with my Spirit and more aware of how positive and negative energy affects our lives. Moreover, he has given me the wisdom and knowledge I have been seeking. The most important gift he has given me is his friendship, not only in the physical world (The NOW), but also in the Spiritual Realm. It is an honor to be a part of Lord DiCaprio life, as well as him a part of mine. Thanks Lord Master Archangel DiCaprio.

"At the presence of the white light I leap, and the joy and happiness follows."

Michael J. Morse

257 In a detention center, since this other lawyer had no clue I was there, until he searched for me.

> *There are certain things that cannot be put into words; however, you have impressed me on how quick to learn you are. You have advanced much faster than I hoped for, and that is why I am proud to call you a friend as well as my brother. All I want from you is to give the next person the love of hope and True Freedom, as I have given you.*
>
> *The calm and balanced mind is strong while the hurried and agitated mind is weak. Fear turns strength to weakness. Everything has to do with attitude and viewpoint. You are made of the same stuff as G—d. Seek the Truth and you shall find it.*

Gino DiCaprio

II. Must I Say More

Here are some quotations from the book by Gracie Karlene Baxter:

> *"You'll know if a Spiritual wisdom is pure and connected" if, as you learn, you catch yourself saying, "Wow, I already knew this. I always felt these truths somewhere deep inside of me. I just didn't know how to articulate them."*
>
> *"You'll know that the 72 names of God are not about religion. In fact, God never created religion. Humans did."*

According to Kabbalah, humans were created with two distinct aspects to their nature—darkness and light. The darkness is the human ego—as in Everybody's Got One. This is where the light hides.

> *"Conflict, intolerance, and darkness cannot, by definition, exist in the presence of Light and true spirituality."*

In light of this statement, perhaps this is how we lost our Spiritual connection. So when I began experiencing a lot of conflict, and dark days, as stated above, this could not exist in the presence of Light and true spirituality. I can see the deepness of this now. You wouldn't say this, but I do remember you saying you couldn't be around negative people; so I was so afraid to tell you about a lot of what was happening with me because I didn't want to lose the connection I had with you. I always received so much positive Spiritual energy from talking with you. But, you dealt with me as patiently as you could, and acted as though it wasn't a problem for you, when in all actuality, it was. Is my understanding of this correct? Thank you for being patient with me until I could reach this point. Thank you so much for not just dismissing me totally.

"It's like turning on the light in a dark room. These forces empower us to completely change our lives and absolutely transform our world." "The light is the human soul, which is obscured by the ego. You see, the ego is not actually you. You just think it's you. But it's really an external garment, a curtain that hides the light of your soul, your true self." (As you would say, what you see is not real, it is an illusion.)

When I let my problems take over my life, it put me back into darkness, even with my faith in God. I began to experience dark days that would totally overwhelm me and cause panic attacks. This has been a vicious cycle for me. When one problem comes the others come back on me like a flood. I often wondered why me? I often wondered if it would ever stop. I suppose when I would pray for help, I didn't realize that I could have the power to escape from my situation on my own. But with this newfound understanding of negative energy and positive energy, darkness and light, my life is taking on a new meaning.

"Each time you allow your ego to control your behavior, and your relations with other people; another curtain is suspended concealing the light of your soul. This is called Reactive Behavior—you react to

the impulse of the ego. Each time you resist your ego, you tear down a curtain. This is called Proactive Behavior—you stop your reflective egocentric impulses and unleash the proactive will of your soul. Life gets brighter."

"Your career, your family, and your friends are here for one purpose—to provide opportunities for you to carry out your personal transformation. They give you a chance to let go of your ego, selfishness, and envy and, in turn, find the light!"

"There are two ways to remove the curtains that obscure the light of the soul: suffering or spiritual transformation. That's all. There are no other options."

I've looked in my book, and right away, I've figured out the way to present the Spiritual Wisdom of Kabbalah, which is the oldest wisdom in the world tracking back 4000 years. It began with Abraham, the father of three great monotheistic religions: Judaism, Christianity, and Islam. Abraham recognized that there were two spheres that affect our lives: spiritual and physical. He revealed the laws for both of these spheres—a code of laws for the workings of the entire universe.

Cracking the Code

Kabbalah says, "*The Bible is a complete code. It's a cryptogram. When this biblical code is cracked, something wonderful happens; awesome spiritual forces are suddenly released into our souls and discharged into the world at large. It's like turning on the light in a dark room. These forces empower us to completely change our lives, and absolutely transform our world. But when the Bible remains coded, read and taken literally (as it has been for some 2000 years), it becomes a fruitless symbol of religious tradition instead of the awesome instrument of power it was meant to be*".

A prime example on an encoded story is the account of Moses and the Israelites and the Red Sea. When they cried out for help and God asked "*Why are you calling out to me*", it was merely a code. God was actually telling the people that they themselves had the power to escape from their perilous predicament on their own.

According to the book, "*The 72 Names of God—Technology for the Soul: The key to this universal law is the offering of true Light and unconditional kindness*".

> *"The reason is unconditional love and authentic Light immediately penetrate the soul of the other party, awakening love and Light in return".*

If that prerequisite is met, all forms of hatred, conflict, and hostility must vanish as quickly as a lit light bulb banishes darkness from a room.

> *"If this doesn't happen, then make no mistake, it wasn't genuine Light that was being shared; there was a hidden agenda behind the love that was offered; there were strings attached to the kindness that was given. It wasn't unconditional. If your effort at peacemaking is not 100 percent sincere, if there's a hidden agenda or speck of self—interest, then this conditional love never reaches the other person's soul. No love is awakened. In other words, it's merely one ego communicating to another."*

So how do you arouse true Light?

How do you awaken the soul?

Easy! The same way you bring light to a darkened room. Simply flip on the switch.

Now, let me compliment you on how you did this for me. Same thing:

Light—Positive energy; Darkness—Negative Energy.

I have been disciplining myself. I ponder these things in my Spirit. I had a negative thought once that you had put me on shut down. You limited the time we talked. It was my fault and my ego, self—centered self that always wanted to talk to you, and I slipped back into darkness, but only for a little while. I'm getting better. I'm growing up! I realize I was looking for light in all the wrong places.

I'm trying to do self—help. I'm learning and everything I'm learning is making me a better person and making my life brighter. It also helps me to see the Light and embrace the positive. So as much as I want to talk with you more, I make an effort not to. It's only fair. I do love, you know, and my love is divine and **UNCONDITIONAL**.

I try to remain positive and use that energy towards myself. It's a day by day, step by step experience. I'm glad to be able to share this learning experience with you and it makes me feel good that you appreciate it.

When I grow up I'm going to be just like you!

You really have done an awesome job. People are either going to believe or disbelieve. They have the option to study for themselves. People are also going to be jealous of you. They will think they can do it better than you.

"The energy that drives this ancient technology comes from these three verses and their 72 letters. The 72 names of God are not 'names' in any ordinary sense. They have nothing in common with what you and I call ourselves. The 72 names of God provide us with a vehicle to connect to the infinite spiritual current that flows through reality.

God gave this cutting edge to Moses to be shared with all people, so that humans could unleash their own God—like powers and attain control over the physical world".

In fact God never answers prayers. It is people who answer their own prayers by knowing how to connect to and utilize the divine energy of the Creator and the God—like force in their own souls.

How's that for a complete paradigm shift?

They were gripped by fear, but Moses reminded them of the 72 names. They began to meditate upon them, employing all their mental powers to arouse breathing spiritual forces.

But you know what, not a single water molecule moved until the Israelites conquered their doubts and waded into the sea with total certainty. Not one drop shifted until they were neck—deep in the sea. Then, when the waters reached their nostrils, and they still maintained complete certainty—swoosh—the waters parted, giving them passage to freedom.

What's the lesson?

"To seize control over the laws of Mother Nature one must attain self—mastery".

Therein lies the secret to the 72 names of God.

But before you can master human nature, you need to know a little bit more about it.

I think this is awesome wisdom and knowledge.

Gracie Karlene Baxter

Thank you very much for you humble letter and most of your points I can agree with. I just want others to know that I am not a religious person whatsoever. I am A Spiritual Warrior who is intertwined with the Universal Consciousness.

Gino DiCaprio

III. As Humans

We are brought up in the world of money, fashion, virtually any thing that you might see on TV, or heard from someone who saw it on TV. Our whole belief system brings us to grow up wanting only one thing, Money...

We can't do this because of ******.

We *need* more ******** to do this.

I can't seem to get enough ********.

What if it's all just a lie?

A huge majority of people are being misled and trained like sheep, to be closed minded, and to conform to the laws that we have been taught.

But has anyone actually stopped and asked why we are all here?

If you go to the right core, to the absolute core, the whole world, even the air around us, is made of atoms, protons, neutrons, and electrons. So if you really stop to think about it, everything is the same thing, and is connected in a way.

The world, as we see it now, are just atoms and vibrations (energy).

If everything is connected, then the simple fact of picturing something would actually create the exact same molecule composition of the photo in your brain, but it's in your brain.

How is that even possible?

This is what I believe: everything is connected and you create your own world. The center of all these thought waves will align itself to create **YOUR REALITY AS YOU PICTURE IT**.

Never doubt yourself, you have Infinite potential!

This Book I: Secrets and Laws of the Universe is a very profound discussion of this inner power we possess, seek your truth, find your answers, and you will believe, like I do now.

Remember, every one is entitled to their own reality. Never wish bad, always bless with luck!

Thank you Lord Gino DiCaprio.

From the Heart and the Brain.

James Bradley

Thank you, James, for your heart felt point of view. I have seen you transform from a very disturb and angry person to becoming a very calm and non—judgemental person. I am honoured and grateful to have met you.

Peace and Love

Gino DiCaprio

Epilogue: Revised

"Forget tomorrow to do what you said, but do it now in the moment in case tomorrow does not come." — **Gino Iovannone**

I have realized the importance of having my books finished. To meet my objectives, I had to accomplish this. I had to schedule myself and wanted to keep the schedule that was put in place. I have worked hard to discipline myself to write this book along with the others I have written, and to keep moving forward when everything around me seemed to be pulling me back. I have worked hard to build my ability to keep my mind, body, and emotions in balance no matter what was happening around me. I have stayed focused and not allowed myself any interruptions or delays. I succeeded by consciously and continuously choosing to act as a disciplined person.

What about you?

No aspect of discipline is more important than keeping an agreement, doing exactly what we have said we would do, exactly when we said we would do it.

Effectiveness by definition requires managing the use of your time, including the time you spend each day getting from one place to another. There are only two times a day when I seem to get sudden flashes of insight, ideas that might be lost if not immediately captured. Those times are late at night or when I am on my way somewhere, while driving. These are the best of times to have a pen and paper around me to record my thoughts.

EPILOGUE: REVISED

I mention in my "*Acknowledgments*" that how I speak and write is very different to from how I used to speak and write, and I want to elaborate on this. With my writing, I am required to punctuate and use grammar correctly. On paper, I am more concise than I am in conversation. What is great about writing is you can always go back and change what you originally wrote or add more, while with on the spot conversation, you cannot go back and add to what you said at that moment.

On stage or with a one—on—one with you, I might not turn a clever phrase and you may not catch it the first time. But, with the written word, you can go back and re—read it all over again. When writing, you are required to be more focussed and concentrated. The idea of those who write books is a dream of immortality. I am sure that you expect a lot from this book, so I made sure that I slowed down my words, because I do talk faster than you could listen with all my stutters and lisps.

I want you to take a few minutes and close your eyes; ask yourself this question:

How do I feel right now as opposed to before I read this book?

I hope you realized that you are more aware and present now then you were before you read my book(s). If not, I did not do a good job because I want to see tremendous progress in you. My job is not to dull your competitive edge, but to sharpen it. What I want is to see that you find yourself effortlessly acting in a more appropriate, efficient, and productive way. So do not be afraid. My book(s) will help you move ahead. I am hoping that you will incorporate some of my teachings into your life by making them part of your daily routine, just like taking your morning shower or brushing your teeth.

I will soon have my personal instruction on video[258] or YouTube with other suggestions. As a result, I know it will build you up and transform your life into a richer experience. Be sure to pick them up, you will be glad you did.

You must fully understand that if you do not "*ask*" for something "*precisely*," you will not get anything "*precisely*", nor should you assume that you will. You ought to fully understand that anything you think of, anything you dream of, "*will*" and can become "*real*" if you "*believe*" it with all your heart, mind and soul, without feeling any doubt whatsoever. You have to fully understand what you want in "*detail*", and demand it. You must want, feel, smell, sense, and taste it like it is already in your hands, NOW. Do not let your negative thoughts and emotions get in the way of what you "*want*". Learn to always think in the "*now*", not in the past or the future, but compress time as one timeline. Always remember that at one time, what you now have was once only a dream. In addition, whatever you imagine can and "*will*" be "*real*" and be "*reality*". Get into the "*habit*" of "*believing*" until you "*receive*" it.

Never underestimate yourself and the gift of aligning yourself with the Universe. Write down all your wishes in "*details*". Do not try, just do it.

Bring your wishes and your dreams under your control for you are "*creating*" in your mind whatever you think. If you doubt your thoughts, you will only increase the chances of "*creating*" an experience you are subconsciously avoiding which becomes self—prophecies. Clear your mind with positive thoughts no matter how unreal your wishes may seem, until you no longer doubt your wishes and dreams. Once you accept that it can be "*real*", and "*believe*" it without any shadow of a doubt whatsoever in your mind, heart and soul… you will "*receive*" it. Your mind cannot hold on to both positive and negative thoughts at the same time, so you must choose which you want. You see, this means

258 CD, DVD, HD DVD and Blu—ray

"*believe*" what you want to see and "believe" that rather than what is "really" there. What is real can be unreal and what is unreal be real.

At this point, you have read about some of the techniques and knowledge in getting your life, time, and confidence under your control. Your energy is important. Get involved and practice what was shown to you so that you can receive your reward. Accomplishing and achieving your dreams is a goal you want to reach. You will create a new way of life and not look back. You will keep all of your attention focused on staying positive as well as staying in control, day by day, step by step, towards your wishes you have set up for yourself. You will use what you have learned in my book(s) that was given to me from a Higher Universal Source, time and time again until it becomes a habit. You will use what appears as a failure to bring you where you want to go. You build your self—confidence to a higher level and double your effectiveness in life. Learn to control "who" you are, your time, experiences, events and emotions that happens around you. You will reach the success you want. **ASK** — **BELIEVE** — and you will **RECEIVE**.

What I have written has to do with my observation as well as experiences I personally had, have seen, and read upon. I have written this to help you by using my experiences. You will do whatever you want with all you read, for it will be your choice how you handle it. One thing I have learned is that I have never met anyone who is not living the life they want, by just reading their attitude. Remember you cannot be me nor can I be you. You are required to find how you click along with what works for you.

Your choice is exceedingly important, for it indicates your call for a certain degree of self—esteem. Egotism cannot connect you with the Universe. Someone who lacks strength of character, as well as self—esteem, will be unable to overcome obstacles that may obstruct their way. Humility and pride do not go together.

Pride and self—esteem do not always stem from self—concern, nor are they always the result of an individual's perception of their personal virtues. A positive self—image and feeling of self—esteem flows naturally from a healthy outlook on life. The very fact that you exist is reason enough for you to experience your self—worth.

These feelings are enhanced by your awareness of the connection you have in being intertwined with the "*Universal Laws of Creation*". Self—centered pride is limited by the finite scope of one's qualities and can be dampened by a formidable challenge or individual. No obstacle can or should be able to stand in your way. Loyalty, honour, and respect are the most important aspect in life.

Do not mis—quote me, however, most people I know are financially successful and working on different projects. A few of my friends have offered me to work for them for a huge amount of money with a three year guarantee and I've turned them down, since my work[259] is more important then losing myself in a job. I know and they know that in the long term what I am doing will bring me more than they can ever offer me, both Spiritually and financially. I have prioritized my commitment. I believe in this mission and adventure.

I will not lie. At the moment I am broke. Thanks to the support of my true friends, my children and ex—wife I am happily broke. I chose to be, so that I can show people how to make it. Money is not my focus. Money will come when it should, and it's a physical need, which I feel is not important at this moment. As I mention, it's the long term goal that is important. This book along with book 2 and 3 explains it too a "*Tee*".

There are certain things I do not let my successful friends be a part of. That is why I am looking for private investors and sponsors who see the potential in what I have to offer.

259 This Mission

Focusing on money is a temporary gratification. True success is when you do not focus on material wealth, but focus on having a life full of adventure. Only at that moment will you truly achieve the success you wanted and wake—up with "*both*" material and Spiritual wealth as such people like Tony Robbins. I have never been a student of his, yet I have read what other big name entertainers say about him helping their career to advance.

The message which my Higher—Self through my Spiritual Guide wants to deliver is for you to focus and enjoy this physical life and where you want it to lead. Most of you are easily distracted instead of paying close attention of your surroundings.

I want to help you create a break—through in your life by maximizing your true abilities.

"I am waiting for people to seek me instead of me seeking them."

Chronicle order of Gino DiCaprio's (formerly Jake Hollow) works:

"Dating Coach"
(with a little touch of the Universal Law of Creation)
By Jake Hollow

~

"The Jake Hollow Guide on How to Persuade Women"
Jake Hollow's "*How to Deal with Emotions and the Life of a Motivational Speaker*"

~

"The Universal Law of Creation: When You Seek, Ask, See and Truly Believe Beyond Any Shadow of a Doubt Whatsoever, You Shall Receive!"
By Gino DiCaprio

~

Book I "Secrets and Laws of the Universe"
Book II: "Time is an Illusion"
Book III: "Illuminatis The Ones and The Shadows"

CPSIA information can be obtained at www.ICGtesting.com
Printed in the USA
LVOW05s0842271213

367048LV00004B/472/P